theatre & the digital

Theatre &
Series Editors: Jen Harvie and Dan Rebellato

Published
Susan Bennett: *Theatre & Museums*
Bill Blake: *Theatre & the Digital*
Colette Conroy: *Theatre & the Body*
Emma Cox: *Theatre & Migration*
Jill Dolan: *Theatre & Sexuality*
Helen Freshwater: *Theatre & Audience*
Jen Harvie: *Theatre & the City*
Nadine Holdsworth: *Theatre & Nation*
Erin Hurley: *Theatre & Feeling*
Dominic Johnson: *Theatre & the Visual*
Joe Kelleher: *Theatre & Politics*
Ric Knowles: *Theatre & Interculturalism*
Caoimhe McAvinchey: *Theatre & Prison*
Bruce McConachie: *Theatre & Mind*
Lucy Nevitt: *Theatre & Violence*
Helen Nicholson: *Theatre & Education*
Lourdes Orozco: *Theatre & Animals*
Lionel Pilkington: *Theatre & Ireland*
Paul Rae: *Theatre & Human Rights*
Dan Rebellato: *Theatre & Globalization*
Trish Reid: *Theatre & Scotland*
Nicholas Ridout: *Theatre & Ethics*
Rebecca Schneider: *Theatre & History*
Fintan Walsh: *Theatre & Therapy*
David Wiles: *Theatre & Time*
Harvey Young: *Theatre & Race*

Forthcoming
Jim Davis: *Theatre & Entertainment*
Eric Weitz: *Theatre & Laughter*

Theatre&
Series Standing Order ISBN 978−0−230−20327−3

You can receive future titles in this series as they are published by placing a
standing order. Please contact your bookseller or, in case of difficulty, write
to us at the address below with your name and address, the title of the series
and the ISBN quoted above.

Customer Services Department, Macmillan Distribution Ltd, Houndmills,
Basingstoke, Hampshire, RG21 6XS, UK

---

theatre & the digital

Bill Blake

palgrave
macmillan

First published 2014 by
PALGRAVE MACMILLAN

Palgrave Macmillan in the UK is an imprint of Macmillan Publishers Limited, registered in England, company number 785998, of Houndmills, Basingstoke, Hampshire RG21 6XS.

Palgrave Macmillan in the US is a division of St Martin's Press LLC, 175 Fifth Avenue, New York, NY 10010.

Palgrave Macmillan is the global academic imprint of the above companies and has companies and representatives throughout the world.

Palgrave® and Macmillan® are registered trademarks in the United States, the United Kingdom, Europe and other countries

ISBN: 978–1–137–35577–5 paperback

This book is printed on paper suitable for recycling and made from fully managed and sustained forest sources. Logging, pulping and manufacturing processes are expected to conform to the environmental regulations of the country of origin.

A catalogue record for this book is available from the British Library.

A catalog record for this book is available from the Library of Congress.

Printed in China.

contents

series editors' preface

The theatre is everywhere, from entertainment districts to the fringes, from the rituals of government to the ceremony of the courtroom, from the spectacle of the sporting arena to the theatres of war. Across these many forms stretches a theatrical continuum through which cultures both assert and question themselves.

Theatre has been around for thousands of years, and the ways we study it have changed decisively. It's no longer enough to limit our attention to the canon of Western dramatic literature. Theatre has taken its place within a broad spectrum of performance, connecting it with the wider forces of ritual and revolt that thread through so many spheres of human culture. In turn, this has helped make connections across disciplines; over the past fifty years, theatre and performance have been deployed as key metaphors and practices with which to rethink gender, economics, war, language, the fine arts, culture and one's sense of self.

Theatre & is a long series of short books which hopes to capture the restless interdisciplinary energy of theatre and performance. Each book explores connections between theatre and some aspect of the wider world, asking how the theatre might illuminate the world and how the world might illuminate the theatre. Each book is written by a leading theatre scholar and represents the cutting edge of critical thinking in the discipline.

We have been mindful, however, that the philosophical and theoretical complexity of much contemporary academic writing can act as a barrier to a wider readership. A key aim for these books is that they should all be readable in one sitting by anyone with a curiosity about the subject. The books are challenging, pugnacious, visionary sometimes and, above all, clear. We hope you enjoy them.

Jen Harvie and Dan Rebellato

foreword

Discussing theatre and the digital is a bit like discussing theatre and electricity. Without qualification and explication it leaves us floundering in a sea of possibilities. Now that an average medium-scale production of *Oklahoma!* employs more computing power than sent a rocket to the Moon, it is fair to say that 'the digital' is so embedded as to become invisible. And yet to attempt to define the digital is a fruitless task – one that Bill Blake wisely sidesteps in this book.

This is a classic example of the problem Wittgenstein identified in *Philosophical Investigations*. When exploring the slipperiness of language he discusses the impossibility of arriving at a precise definition of games. Any attempt to produce a cast-iron rule – games must be fun, or have goals, or rules or a specified outcome – is immediately out-witted by the example of a game that is not fun, or does not have goals, or rules or a fixed outcome. Wittgenstein develops the idea of 'family resemblance' instead. No game may meet all the conditions but each game will meet most of them and thus we can all readily understand what a game is despite the lack of a dependable definition that applies in all circumstances.

When we consider the digital in the context of theatre, it may be most productive to focus in on the most significant and disruptive elements that it brings to bear on the artform. Theatre has prized itself as an interactive artform, especially in opposition to the cinema and television as each technological upstart usurped the stage from which it sprang. However, the most significant characteristic of the 'digital revolution' is an explosive new amount of interaction and participation that is profoundly different in volume and character from what has gone before. It poses new challenges for theatre that are only beginning to be understood. It offers new audiences and new communities. And it demands new forms of performance and new spaces to show it in.

In *The Empty Space* Peter Brook writes that 'a man walks across [a bare stage] whilst someone else is watching him, and that is all that is needed for an act of theatre to be engaged'. Those four fundamental theatrical particles that Brook identifies – the performer, the audience member, at this particular place and in this particular time – are all challenged in a world that is networked.

In an online space such as a chat room or a virtual world, the line between audience and performer is blurred and may shift from one moment to the next. Even in a physical space a work like *Rider Spoke* by Blast Theory invites each 'audience member' to participate as a performer and co-author in the work: the recordings you make as you cycle through the city become the text for participants who come after you. In her research Sherry Turkle has elegantly explored the multiple ways in which online identity is representational, malleable and hard to grasp.

In telematics, two physically separate spaces can be joined together to make a new hybrid. The Mixed Reality Lab at the University of Nottingham is one of the research centres that has explored what the new boundaries within and between virtual spaces might look like. Station House Opera regularly link remote cities to create a new hybrid stage. Chatroulette allows anyone with internet access to be video linked to a random stranger anywhere on Earth.

And in so doing, the wrinkles of networked time become increasingly apparent. My 'now' is not the same as your 'now'. Whether intentionally delayed (as TV broadcasters do regularly) or simply held up by that pesky fibre connection that adds milliseconds to your intercontinental journey, there is a temporal separation when a network connection is made. Sometimes this is apparent, at other times hidden, but it is more than just a technical hurdle.

Even when there is no hardware limit to instantaneous connection, every digital platform has its own affordances and time cycles. Watching a live video stream on a tablet is a different experience to watching the same stream in a cinema. Even though both are ostensibly real time, we expect message responses on SMS to be quicker than on Twitter, for example. When platforms such as these enter the dramaturgical space they bring their own forms of 'now' with them.

When extrapolated over decades these small examples point towards radical challenges for theatre. If theatre is truly to be the artform of interaction and participation, then we must ask ourselves these questions and be ready to follow the thrilling thread of live performance wherever it may lead.

Matt Adams co-founded Blast Theory, a four-times BAFTA-nominated group renowned for its pioneering mix of art, games and theatre. Matt has curated at Tate Modern and at the ICA in London. He is a visiting professor at the Central School of Speech and Drama, University of London, UK.

theatre & the digital

Theatre as we know it is 'undergoing life-threatening mutations'; the whole culture of drama and theatre, according to Michael Kustow, a former associate director of the National Theatre in London and the Royal Shakespeare Company, is about to be 'subsumed by webs and networks' (*theatre@risk*, 2001, p. xiii). Or, coming from a similarly alarmist but entirely more hopeful perspective, the actor and academic Matthew Causey believes we are on the cusp of a 'revolution of historical proportions': he predicts that in discovering the 'uniquely performative qualities' of digital environments, we will come to embrace a 'new aesthetics of the virtual', and in that way the theatre will eventually become revitalized as an all-purpose 'metaphysical laboratory for the exploration of our humanity' (*Theatre and Performance in Digital Culture: From Simulation to Embeddedness*, 2006, pp. 60, 61). More broadly still, cognitive researcher and theatre scholar Nicola Shaughnessy

1

contends that our everyday experiences in the digital world have already altered 'how we perceive and conceptualize' reality, both in life and in art, transforming the very conditions of possibility for 'live' performance (*Applying Performance: Live Art, Socially Engaged Theatre and Affective Practice*, 2012, p. xx). But this too might actually turn out to be for the good: taking a similar line, Baz Kershaw, a stage-design engineer, director, and cultural activist, encourages us to view 'the digital age not as a threat to live theatre but as a possible source of its rebirth and enhancement in a new kind of sensorium' (*Theatre Ecology: Environments and Performance Events*, 2008, p. 73). Finally, regardless of such theorizing and prediction among theatre artists and scholars, recent evidence suggests that audiences themselves might already be on the other side of this digital revolution: a 2010 report commissioned by the Royal National Theatre found that audiences who watched plays in a digitally mediated form – streamed live at a local movie theatre, or online on their own personal computers – experienced 'even higher levels of emotional engagement with the production than audiences at the theatre' (Hasan Bakhshi, Juan Mateos-Garcia, and David Throsby, *Beyond Live: Digital Innovation in the Performing Arts*, p. 2). All these different attitudes and convictions about the relation between theatre and the digital make for a heady mix of alarmism and wilfulness, inevitability and hope. To imagine that the theatre may be on the verge of giving itself up to the digital amounts to either the worst possible threat or a much-desired revolutionary promise.

It is really something new for the theatre to be talked about in these ways. Not that there is anything new in itself about a confrontation between theatre and technology, of course. In the early twentieth century, for instance, many theatre people believed that the radio would soon make live theatre obsolete, or at least bring about such drastic changes that the theatre would become unrecognizable as a distinct art form. Another example: at the turn of the eighteenth century in Europe, it was widely feared that machines and mechanisms were taking over the stage, so much so that technical feats of engineering and spectacle-driven stage design were thought to be supplanting serious drama altogether. Theatre people at the time argued that government needed to step in to subsidize traditional theatre (a familiar plea still today) in order to prevent it from being overrun by popular melodrama and gaudy musicals; otherwise, the expectation was that drama would end up becoming an exclusively literary art form, found in books and perhaps in the drawing room, but never again existing as a properly public art, meaningfully performed (also a familiar complaint today – though substitute universities and urban basements for the drawing room, and obviously forget about the idea that dramatic works might find new life in the hands of a literary reading public).

To be sure, you could argue that the theatre always has been and always will be under threat from technology. In fact, if your faith in theatre – an old faith, still strongly held by many – is based on the ideal of unmediated artistic experience and expression (live, intimate, immediate,

embodied), then you pretty much need the threat of technological change as a backdrop against which to assert your
claims about theatre's specialness. The digital – cyberspace,
information webs, social media, computational processes,
electronic representation, and so on – is nearly perfect for
this purpose. Live interaction, genuine intimacy, real presence, and bodily expression are all exactly what the digital
lacks, and indeed often seems to suggest we could just as
well do without. The opposition between theatre and the
digital, in this formulation, is neither new nor unexpected.

Even so, it is hard to shake the impression that something completely new is at stake here. What are we to make
of the particular balance between the types of claim already
noted above? On the one side, the concern is that this time
the theatre is not just at risk of being changed, but on the
threshold of disappearing altogether. On the other side, we
find all sorts of equally sweeping assertions that by embrac-
ing the digital, we may be near to fulfilling many of theatre's most fundamental aspirations, and opening the way to
even greater aspirations as yet unimagined. Two outlooks,
both holistic and absolute: annihilation, or else progress.

The promise of something different

This book is about a theatre that does not shrink from taking up the cause of whole-scale arts progress and cultural
liberation. The threat of annihilation is far less interesting,
as the increasingly marginal status of traditional theatre
would seem to make such fears both obvious and belated.
Inversely, staring down what we are likely to have in sight as

a hopeless endgame and turning it into the opening gambit of a liberation narrative – there is a lot to say about that, both as a sign of our times and as a historical problem for our future.

My main thesis, then, is that under the aegis of the digital (a completely unspecific concept that nonetheless – or therefore – gives the sense of the particularly momentous) the terms of intellectual communication about the theatre are rapidly changing. The theatre arts are changing as well, of course, as the arts always do. But the more significant change is not a matter of innovative cultural production (new works of art), but a fundamental rethinking of the cultural project. The notion that there is such a thing as a coherent theatre-cultural project and the belief that it can be rethought, and by way of that reconfigured, are in themselves examples of this new progress-seeking strain of discourse about the theatre.

Some might find any such talk of progress even more alarming than the real fact of crisis. The critique of utopian delusions of progress and mastery has, in fact, long been a staple of the theatrical avant-garde. 'The essence of theater', the apostate theatre theorist Antonin Artaud writes, 'lies for us in an imponderable quality that does not accommodate itself in any way to progress' (*Selected Writings*, 1976, p. 158). The rejection of progress in this vein is compelled by a revolt against rationalism and science, more particularly the twin values of control and domination. A cultivation of artistic faith is often presented as the obvious alternative: the pursuit of an 'imponderable quality', achieved only by chance – or, as Artaud insists, 'a single miracle would be sufficient reward for our efforts and our patience' (p. 158). This sometimes spoken, sometimes unspoken logic of miracles, fortitude, and faith explains why the whole theatre culture can be failing – bad plays, alienated audiences, critical neglect – and the theatre arts can still be deemed on pace for success. Artaud again: 'I am not one of those who believe that civilization has to change in order for the theatre to change' (p. 256). Cultural change neither predicts nor determines artistic invention. A striking work of ingenious invention lies outside our control, even beyond our will; artistic success is a gift, not a promise.

The contrast between a faith-based (anti-progress) and a rationalized (progress-seeking) arts culture brings out the problem of the relationship between the part – the individual work, the individual artist, and so on – and the whole – the theatre-cultural project at large. Why have a theatre culture at all? In what ways does our society acknowledge the value of theatre as an autonomous activity? How do those societal values compare with the more specific values of theatre artists?

The idea of progress in the arts

The goal of improving the nature and status of theatre tends to rest on the conviction that a deepening of values at the wide level of artistic, social, cultural, and political purpose can guide the making of better works of theatre. A better work of theatre, following this equation, is anything that realizes – or even just strives to realize – a better world, as defined at the outset by the artist's or theatre company's deep statement of values. Those same values are also meant to influence and predict how audiences receive the work, as well as to decide more long-term matters related to preservation, dissemination, revival, adaptation, and further advancement. A broad but intense sense of purpose and direction propels arts innovation and cultural participation forward towards progress. The 'digital', as we will see, is an excellent fuel for exactly such propulsion.

Particularly important in our digital moment are values associated with the global, plural, and inclusive. Greater artistic freedom, increased audience involvement and access, further engaged civic commitments – in the context of the digital, there is something newly obvious about such concerns among theatre artists and producers, theatregoers and critics, arts supporters and cultural policy makers. In any case, what is ultimately arrived at is a whole view of the theatre-cultural enterprise in which all elements of theatrical production and reception appear as though they can be rationalized and explained. Take, for example, the multiplying objectives that the Vancouver-based Electric Company Theatre claim in their artistic mission statement:

> We strive to produce theatre that is life affirming, inspiring, and provocative. Our work transports audiences to the frontiers of art, knowledge, and human experience. We believe in theatre that is accessible financially and thematically. Our projects cross artistic disciplines and integrate

new media. ... We work to reach across cultures, backgrounds, economics, and ideology to find the universal elements that connect all members of our community. ('Mission & History', electriccompanytheatre.com/company/mission-history/)

At least three coterminous strata of generalities are involved in these remarkable assertions: a strong cultural belief in broad liberal values ('life affirming', 'inspiring', 'accessible'), a creative practice that combines theatre and the digital ('our projects cross artistic disciplines and integrate new media'), and a mission that assumes purposefulness on all fronts of the theatrical enterprise (arts innovation, audience inclusiveness, community outreach, economic viability, ideology critique, and so forth). Interestingly – and not incidentally – this rhetoric of progress overflows into the central ideas of the Electric Company's plays as well: 'Invention, the obsession to change the world, the impulse to create, the spirit of the pioneer and the danger and promise of the frontier have been recurring themes in much of our work' (ibid.). Both the Electric Company's overall mission and their primary subject of artistic exploration draw on the same general principles of innovation and entrepreneurialism.

Such coherence of practical endeavour and creative engagement could not be more at odds with the avant-gardist faith in the 'single miracle' discussed above, where an uncertain achievement of unpredictable insight motivates a more grasping form of artistic pursuit. From this outlook, it could be said that the part subsumes the whole. Effectively, the larger enterprise of the theatre arts is justified on the sole basis of a 'striking and ingenious invention' (Artaud, *Selected Writings*, p. 158). Far from making any claims to universal purposefulness, the avant-gardist holds that an avowal of mere persistence is sufficient. It is unnecessary to demonstrate a record of past success: the debris of failed efforts simply confirms the greater will of the expressive self.

The arts critic Maggie Nelson, a recent proponent of these views, admits to the constant test of faith involved in the 'bumper-car style' randomness of navigating between good works and bad. 'Staying onboard for such a ride', Nelson explains, 'can generate a good amount of ambivalence, volatility, attraction, and repulsion. Some of this, I enjoy. Much — perhaps most — I do not. Nonetheless, I persist' (*The Art of Cruelty*, 2011, p. 10). In a way, Nelson transposes the individual wilfulness of the striving artist into her self-image as a persistent seeker of good art. Moreover, whereas theatre entrepreneurs like the Electric Company Theatre might declare themselves to be committed integrationists ('reach across cultures', 'find the universal elements', 'connect all members of our community'), Nelson proceeds on the assumption of disintegration. As she sees it, there is no way to predict any pattern of good theatre making, let alone to guarantee any effective programme of outreach and impact. Even a successful work is likely to be uneven in its qualities, and, regardless, the measure of success is mainly a 'gut feeling', which of course differs for each gut. A good work can only be defined as 'one of those I-know-it-when-I-see-it type of things' (p. 10). For Nelson, the only reliable guide to the arts scene is scepticism: 'Whether or not one intends for one's art to express or stir compassion, to address or rectify forms of social injustice, to celebrate or relieve suffering' – all this is ultimately 'irrelevant to its actual effects' (p. 9). We need to rid ourselves of the rationalist, humanist consensus which holds that good intentions and good works of theatre go hand in hand. 'Miracle' moments (Artaud's term) of 'unpredictable insight' (Nelson's phrase) come to those who dedicate themselves to a persistent, instinctual, almost spiritual quest for self-discovery and expressive force. The theatre derives its power, under these terms, from the commitments of the individual, and operates only in particulars. Wide-scale, holistic progress is not only outside the picture; it is also very much the wrong idea.

The digital imperative

Why should the 'digital' bring about ideas of progress in the theatre arts? This question is central to this book's concerns. I should acknowledge straightaway that we will be dealing mainly in implicit trends and less so with professed revolutionary creeds (although there are some of those, too, as the quotes from Causey, Shaughnessy, and Kershaw in the opening paragraph would suggest). But, for me, that makes these considerations all the more pressing and tangible. The new habits of thought that are accruing around the theatre's engagements with the digital are indicative of all sorts of change, in both artistic and entrepreneurial arenas. The conventions for how we articulate arts values and promote our cultural work, for instance, are being reshaped right before our eyes, though much of this reshaping seems to be going unnoticed, or at least unremarked, even by those who happen to adopt the new rhetoric themselves. Accordingly, our discussion will focus on drawing out the cultural assumptions underlying recent digitally related works of theatre and digitally motivated theatre entrepreneurialism. Staying in the realm of cultural negotiations, I will be keeping away from any sort of argument about the techno-historical determination of theatre's future. I will also not be attempting anything like a comprehensive survey of digital theatre, in terms of either the art or the scholarship. The digital, after all, is an ever multiplying and mostly impossible-to-pin-down referent, with the meanings and cultural conceptions of new media and 'digital culture' multifarious and elusive. What our theatre culture is responding to with respect to the digital is just as uncertain as how it is responding. On-the-ground negotiations such as those discussed in this book do not, therefore, have the advantage of settled outcomes or even agreed-upon terms of debate. But what our titular keyword may lack in concreteness, it gives back by allowing us to concern ourselves with general problems and big questions. Indeed, under the auspices of the digital, I will argue, the scope of the questions we are asking about theatre culture and the performing arts has reached a new order of magnitude, and that in itself is worthy of closer thought.

Whenever the term 'digital' is brought to bear on a pre-defined subject (in our case, the theatre), it is conventional to immediately point up the non-specificity of the concept. You may have noticed that I have tripped around this issue a few times already. The typical way forward is to define and delimit a particular historical or theoretical focus, while avoiding falling into the gravity well of more precise definitions. The theatre scholar Martin Harries, for instance, argues that it is impossible even to conceive of a relationship between theatre and new media without first framing a 'particular investigation of theatre's place in a particular culture and a particular time' ('Theater and Media before "New" Media', 2012, p. 9). As Harries rightly observes, 'there is no relationship between theatre and new media: there are relationships, contingent and shifting and worth attention to their particularity' (pp. 7–8). With such an understanding in mind, the ampersand of this book's title is a bit of a phoney wager: the pairing of theatre and the digital is a meaningless topic until we have narrowed things down to a case study. At stake is not just the matter of committing to a principle of selection; more essentially, we need to be careful not to treat the digital – or the theatre – as an established and stable object of investigation, either historically or in the present. A constructive analysis of how the theatre relates to the digital must be alert to particularities on both sides of the equation, as well as to the particular context of any particular pairing. This is a useful reminder, especially when we consider all the exaggerations of rhetoric that the 'digital' seems to give rise to.

That having been said, it is in many ways the very fact of those exaggerations of rhetoric that I am most interested in here. A tendency to generalize and overstate what goes on between theatre and audiences – or, more so, theatre and society – is how we end up on the uncertain ground of talking about ideas of progress in the arts. In looking both at cases of digital innovations being applied to the theatre and at examples of plays that are about digital innovations, it is helpful to keep these generalities in direct view. The digital, whether by dint of its technological affordances or its rapid and immense cultural impact, has become uniquely conducive to a discourse featuring sweeping definitions and escalating assumptions. The theatre, as I will show, is both an active contributor to and a specially engaged observer of this discourse.

For these reasons, I plan to leave open the idea of the digital throughout this book, and in some instances push even further at its broad sweeps and grand contours. This is not to suggest that detailed and specific theories of the digital and its relationship to theatre do not exist. Theatre and performance scholars have done much important work on this topic, both complicating and refining the scope of particular concerns. Especially influential has been Hans-Thies Lehmann's thinking about the dynamic 'remediations' between performance and new media. Lehmann identifies this dynamic as a defining feature of what he terms 'post-dramatic theatre' – a theatre that is hyper-theatrical both in its art and in its reception, having given up on any attempt to represent or simulate the real world; instead, its aim is

to achieve an immersive, self-reflexive experience of theatrical time and space (*Postdramatic Theatre*, 2006). The
use of new media, particularly the use of digital projection
technology and live video feeds, contributes to this uniquely
immersive but estranging and disintegrative environment of
postdramatic theatre; 'a space between realities', as Nicola
Shaughnessy positively describes it (*Applying Performance*,
p. 245). Most scholarship on multimedia performance,
accordingly, pays close attention to the interface between
the live and the digital, the real and the virtual. Kurt
Vanhoutte and Nele Wynants, for instance, write about
the richly imaginative, provocative, destabilizing effects of
'being submerged (being present) in an electronically mediated environment' ('Immersion', 2010, p. 47). Jason Farman
further qualifies that it is not just the specific encounter with
technological aspects of multimedia performance, but the
'continual oscillation between the material and the digital
that situates the audience and interactively engages them',
both in the experience of the theatrical event and in the
effort of coming to some meaningful insight into that experience ('Surveillance Spectacles', 2009, p. 182). Whereas
Vanhoutte, Wynants, and Farman reflect on the innovative use of new media technologies within the regular space
of the theatre, Shannon Jackson (*Social Works: Performing
Art, Supporting Publics*, 2011) looks at examples where artists take 'certain theatrical fundamentals' – scripted dialogue and action, personalized characters, an interest in
cultural topics – and creatively interpose those elements
into situations regularly experienced only in the digital

realm: for instance, an intercontinental online video chat with a call-centre worker in Rimini Protokoll's *Call Cutta in a Box* (premiered simultaneously at Willy-Brandt Haus in Berlin, Schauspielhaus in Zurich, and the National Theatre in Mannheim, 2008; www.rimini-protokoll.de/website/en/project_2766.html), or the at-home habit of watching a video or playing a video game, as invoked in London-based motiroti and New York-based The Builders Association's collaborative cross-media performance project *Alladeen* (Wexner Center for the Arts, Columbus, OH, 2003; www.alladeen.com). Alternatively, outside the analysis of innovative works of theatre, scholars have also recently sought to bring certain concepts and analytical approaches from performance theory to bear on the study of social media use and digital practice, including email (Rosemary Klich, 'Send: Act: Perform', 2013; Esther Milne, *Letters, Postcards, Email: Technologies of Presence*, 2010), Twitter (John Muse, '140 Characters in Search of a Theatre: Twitter Plays', 2012), and computer code (Alice Rayner, 'Everywhere and Nowhere: Theatre in Cyberspace', 1999; Anna Munster, *Materialising New Media: Embodiment in Information Aesthetics*, 2006). In all this work, as well as in the work of a fast-growing number of other theatre and performance scholars, including Johannes Birringer, Susan Broadhurst, Maria Chatzichristodoulou, Lars Elleström, Peter Gendolla, Gabriella Giannachi, Josephine Machon, Timothy Murray, Francisco Ricardo, Jörgen Shäfer, and Rachel Zerihan, thinking about the digital in relation to the theatre, and vice versa, has given focus to a wide range of important questions about the aesthetics

of the virtual, the artistic potential of interactive technologies, and the creative possibilities inherent in multimodal
and intermedial forms. Besides this work of conceptual-
izing and theorizing the digital, multimedia performance
scholars are actively capturing, historicizing, and critically
responding to what Steve Dixon identifies as an 'emergent
avant-garde' (*Digital Performance: A History of New Media
in Theater, Dance, Performance Art, and Installation*, 2007,
p. 7). For artists and scholars, the topic of theatre and the
digital spans an energy-rich borderland of theory, while at
the same time giving shape to an impressive postdramatic
heartland of innovative theatre.

From the broader cultural outlook of this book, however, innovative theatrical experiments that make use of
innovative new media technologies are only one of the
many ways in which the digital has become – or seems to
have become – an impetus or motive force for new dis-
courses, new artistic trends, new creative forms, new
entrepreneurial initiatives, new work practices, new institutional arrangements, and new social, political, and cultural aspirations in the theatre arts (of course, many of the
scholars above keenly discuss these issues as well). Because
it is these multiple permutations of the topic of theatre and
the digital that are the subject of this book, in what follows
we will be dealing as much, or more, in baggy, makeshift,
promissory definitions of the digital as we will with well-
developed scholarly concepts and well-known, frequently
studied works of multimedia performance. In fact, the
performance examples we will be looking at most closely

— the Electric Company's multimodal theatre experiment *At Home With Dick and Jane*, the Elevator Repair Service's algorithmically generated performance installation *Shuffle*, Neworld Theatre's PodPlays, and The Mission Business's transmedia experience *ZED.TO* — have all been chosen not because the theatre company (or whoever) has achieved something particularly innovative in their use of the digital, but because the terms in which they cast the *potential* significance of the digital says much about what they perceive the theatre to be and what they are hopeful the theatre will become.

Something else to note in advance: although I make mention of numerous international examples throughout, all my main case studies come from North America, predominantly Canada. Admittedly, this is in part because I happen to be a Canadian who lives and works in New York. As I will show, however, there is also a key set of cultural (and metacultural) contexts — arts funding arrangements, opportunities for cross-institutional partnerships, predictable patterns of cultural participation and community support — common to my selection of case studies, and that commonality holds some significance for my argument. Ultimately, though, the extent to which local factors of cultural geography still matter in a culture of digital flow and global ambitions — most of these works also toured in Europe and Asia, and of course exist online, in one form or another — will become, in the end, just another line of questioning that a short book like this one can only start to open up, and nowhere near answer (the further reading section

17

at the back offers an overview of useful sources for more extensive thinking and research on these topics).

So long as we remain aware that we are discussing attitudes and values, not seeking to determine settled facts or accepted norms, surveying these highly selective examples in an almost associative sequence should be an accessible and rewarding task – an overhearing of potent but unconnected voices of the digital age, as though eavesdropping on the inner ambitions and worries of a dissociated theatre community. There is an argument that I will be making along the way, too, about the idea of progress in the arts, but to avoid overplaying my hand, let me first put a few more cards on the table.

New mediaspeak

'I like the smell of live theatre,' says the theatre director of the Electric Company's *At Home With Dick and Jane* (HIVE 3/Centre for Digital Media, Vancouver, 2010). The live presence of theatre is a valued notion because it appears to be an irreducible one: it is as impossible to produce theatre without liveness as it would be to produce film without mediation. Liveness also provides theatre with a special claim to the real: 'There has never been a *real* film made,' the theatre director of *At Home With Dick and Jane* goes on to assert; in his opinion, film artists 'don't understand the medium they're working in'. He antagonizes the medium of film throughout the interview, even making the point that 'you can't smell actors on film'. Medium constitutes a final reckoning of artistic primacy, for which theatre is prepared to draw its lines.

The giveaways that this is a mock interview come frequently: 'I like that you can smell the actors, in particular their hair,' and so on. As the character of the theatre director mires himself in overloaded art-speak, the interview cuts back and forth to the similarly stupid but not unintelligible art-speak of a female director talking about her film version of *At Home With Dick and Jane*. What distinguishes their statements as empty art-speak is the sheer amount of posturing and pretence, the unwavering sense of artistic self-importance, and the absolute insistence on the primacy of their own medium. After about ten minutes of carefully edited interview footage, we are laughing in particular at their ludicrous assertions about having brought out the 'humanity' and 'presence' of 'such ordinary people', Dick and Jane. Lots of oblique comparison ('Dick is very human, but not as human as Jane'), circular statement ('a living, breathing representation of the natural world'), and meaningless profundity ('my film makes them stranger than they actually were, such that they become ultra-normal') make it easy to recognize all this talk as false and self-pleading. But, without such mockery, how are we otherwise supposed to know the difference between a fake rhetoric of artistic purposefulness and a real statement of purpose?

Audience members were left to watch a digital video of this interview in a small screening-room prior to entering the live performance space. The video piece is entirely in the mode of compulsive mockery, which might be explained by the implied format – a DVD 'extras' interview, with the interviewees shot in front of a black background, answering unspoken questions while looking directly into the camera. The format is distinct for its arch-seriousness; for that reason, it is also distinct for being regularly spoofed. The inclusion of extra material on DVDs came about as a result of the affordances of digital storage: because DVDs were cheap to produce, easy to edit, and capable of storing large amounts of video, it was possible to include more than just the feature film on a single disc, and so more was added. An increase in media storage, or so this argument runs, resulted in an indiscriminate broadening of content. The justification for creating more and more additional content (outpacing actual fan interest in most cases), and the often obsessively self-referential nature of that content, came to seem increasingly suspect. Director interviews – perhaps the least (for me) interesting genre of DVD bonus material, but also probably the most common – allowed a sense of importance to develop, without a clear sense of audience. Self-satire and mock versions provided a necessary counterbalance, as well as being comically entertaining in their own right. The mock interview with the directors of both the theatre and the film versions of *At Home With Dick and Jane* is born of this trend.

It is the juxtaposition of this inessential mediated artspeak with the scene of artisanal, handmade, selfless art making staged in the live theatre portion of the work that provides *At Home With Dick and Jane* with its broader theme. The overall work gains an added complication from how audiences actually view the live performance: after waiting in the screening-room, an audience member – one at a time — takes a seat on a camera dolly chair, and then is pushed along a track while looking through a tiny viewfinder. The experience is one of being behind the camera for a 'live' tracking shot of an ongoing performance. Moving down the track, we first see, through a window, a woman (Jane) examining an unexposed film real. A male hand then appears (this is Dick), tapping at the window. We continue to move along the track, entering through the front door of Dick and Jane's house, into a hallway. Jane is momentarily glimpsed hurrying behind a wall, where she appears to be setting up to spy on Dick with her home video camera through an air vent. Dick enters the main room and sits down by the fire for a bit, all the while being recorded by Jane. He then gets up to go find Jane. He finds her in a bedroom, but just as he enters, she quickly hides the video camera and picks up her knitting. They sit together, laughing, sharing a drink, kissing (an innocent, domestic peck). When Jane gets up to leave, Dick reaches behind a curtain to retrieve a pair of hair scissors he has apparently hidden there for some purpose. We move onwards down the track into the kitchen, where dinner is cooking on the stove; then into the bathroom, where Jane is washing. Unnoticed (by Jane), Dick sneaks up behind her and cuts off a lock of her hair. Finally, we move into the basement, where Dick and Jane are neatly giftwrapping their respective homemade gifts — Dick, a little cloth-doll, presumably with Jane's real hair as its hair; Jane, a reel of home movies, presumably taken of Dick in the house while he is unawares. After opening each other's gifts, they immediately proceed, as if this were a

happy and longstanding routine, to stage a miniature puppet play, with Dick's creation, the cloth-doll, dancing on a
makeshift stage and Jane's reel-to-reel video projected on a
paper screen behind. Across the tiny stage, Dick and Jane
reach out and hold hands. They then dangle a homemade
'Cut' sign to end scene.

Contrasted with the mock interview video, the live portion of *At Home With Dick and Jane* suggests lots of obvious
lessons for our digital age, and some less obvious. The most
straightforward takeaway is that Dick and Jane represent all
that is real and genuine, pure and unadulterated about artistic creativity. Unlike the theatre and film directors in the
interview, Dick and Jane are devoted to an actual craft, not
an assumed concept. They have only themselves as an audience (not including us, but we will get to that in a moment),
so instead of attempting to justify their work to an (imagined) universal audience, and therefore entangling themselves in abstract art-speak and artistic self-promotion, they
are concerned only with their shared love of the art-making
process and the domestic harmony it engenders at home.
The forms of art and the discourse about art that result
from a digitally expanding media platform are corruptions —
of artistic principle, of traditional culture, of basic common
sense. For Dick and Jane, art production is an intimate,
craftsy, habitual, rustic (the 'Cut' sign is made of twigs),
familiar, homely, affectionate practice. Meaningfulness in
art, for them, is indistinguishable from their life principle.
This authentic sensibility is further confirmed by the fact
that Dick and Jane are fully collaborative in their mixed-

media theatre project: their common respect for film (non-digital) and theatre (puppetry) correlates with their selfless exchange of creativity. The mock interview suggests that mixed media divides artists, revealing their narcissism and pointless competitiveness. Dick and Jane, alternatively, prove that mixed media can naturally combine, in the same loving spirit as that which forms their domestic bliss.

Digital unease

A simple division between digital media's corruptive effects and the nostalgic promotion of an artisanal theatre happily cordoned off from those effects – this is one of the lessons *At Home With Dick and Jane* might leave us with. There is something to be said for the recuperative power of such easily expressed instinctive views. To be sure, the opposition drawn here between theatre and the digital is extremely exaggerated, and, after closer thought, questionable both in its principle and in its conception. But for audiences and theatre artists concerned with traditional theatre's apparent marginalization at the hands of the digital, the alternative logic of an artisanal theatre has an obvious appeal. Artisanal theatre – theatre that relies on all its members (including, increasingly, audiences) cooperating at all levels of the company's creative production and entrepreneurial success, and thereby deepening the participants' respect for both the craft and the business of theatre – closely links to the idea of collective responsibility. Although more a reactionary than a revolutionary moral, a new emphasis on liberatory art values still has the potential to change the terms of the perceived problem: in place of the digital's false promise of online connectivity, artisanal theatre, as imagined through analogy with Dick and Jane's homemade theatre work, substitutes an ideal of participatory companionship. In place of reaching outwards to a universal and homogeneous audience, and thereby falling into the trap of vague and artistically insecure art-speak, the craft maker's ethos of artistic practice grounds the theatre in selfless, mutually rewarding purposefulness. No more fussy and ambiguous aesthetics; instead, an immediate and immersive pleasure in the whole process of art making. As a site of collaborative exploration and play, the theatre might well be the perfect context for realizing such artisanal values.

The digital, in this way, prompts a rethinking of core arts values, not determining anything but influential in shaping the overall discussion and compelling a new vision (ironically, *At Home With Dick and Jane* was staged at Vancouver's Centre for Digital Media, whose explicit mission is to make the city 'a leader in the digital media industry'). Even as a background fact – as the source and format of the mockumentary video, and as conspicuous absence in the live documentary of Dick and Jane at home – the digital shows its influence in channelling significant mutations in discourse and cultural practice. But, given how the digital operates as a multiplier of broad themes and anxieties, we should also therefore be aware that the picture is likely to look very different from each different angle.

The easy sentiment of the counter-digital, as demonstrated above, relies on simplified distinctions between the mediated and the real, the technological and the homemade, the universal and the local, the overstated and the unspoken, the endlessly looping and the organically harmonious, the ridiculously pretentious and the authentically purposeful *At Home With Dick and Jane* encourages us to think in terms of this either-or logic, and yet there are strong hints that all this might be a red herring. It is difficult to ignore, for instance, that there is an essential creepiness to Dick and Jane's routine: Jane secretly videotaping Dick's private moments at home and Dick stalking behind Jane with a pair of scissors imbue their homely scene of artistic collaboration with problems of intrusiveness, strangeness, even a degree of sinisterism. The heightened tensions of each trying to keep their own part of the creative project secret from the other, albeit endearing as a trope of gift giving between lovers, are uncomfortable for us to watch. Which raises the question: what exactly are we doing watching this scene, anyway? If some sort of argument for artisanal theatre values is being made, what is the point of us watching from behind the lens of a camera?

Whatever creepiness hangs over the live portion of *At Home With Dick and Jane* comes directly from the fact of our watching. Dick and Jane do not acknowledge our presence, although we might wonder whom they are actually staging their puppet play for, especially given that the miniature stage faces outwards and has both a front curtain and a rear curtain, and therefore also a backstage, where Dick and Jane remain until sharing a final handshake across the stage. The question of audience would seem to be an important one. If we were meant to belittle the rival film and theatre directors for talking narcissistically between themselves, then how do we account for the extreme insularity (in their basement, alone) and mutual obsessiveness (a doll version of Jane, a film about Dick) that equally but differently characterize Dick and Jane's art making? Watching them through the camera's viewfinder serves, at one level, to frame their activities as meaningful: whatever unspoken values they might apply to their own practice, the labelling of those values as intimacy, immediacy, authenticity, and affection belongs primarily to our outsider perspective. Moreover, our sense that they are involved in a special form of art making depends on our recognizing the difference from the mock interview – for instance, that analogue mixed media is to real intimacy as digital-born content is to false competitiveness. Our filmic perspective has us believing in our own take on 'humanity' and 'presence'. Just as the mockumentary video has the effect of pointing up the directors' pretentiousness, the 'real' documentary video that we are behind the camera for is what lends Dick and Jane's scene its preciousness, or at least produces the significance of that preciousness. Interview us, and we are likely to sound just as grasping and overstated in our own desired view of Dick and Jane as 'ultra-normal'.

At another level, then, the effect of watching through the camera lens is not collaborative or contributive at all. Rather the opposite: if we truly believe that what we are witnessing is intimate, then there is an obvious element of intrusiveness on our part. And if we accept that that intimacy is at least partly produced by our documentary gaze, then the actual unease we have with Dick and Jane spying on and stalking each other should probably lead us to call into question the mediated basis on which all our positive beliefs about art making and cultural production rest.

Curiously, the film director in the mock interview seems to anticipate exactly this dilemma. 'I find a live theatre audience feels embarrassed for themselves', she admits, 'and embarrassed for the performers.' Our filmic perspective, it could be said, is the only thing preventing the scene from transforming into absolute strangeness and, potentially, danger. The constitutive elements of the scene, after all, include spying, stalking, sex, sacrifice, fanaticism, and ritual. If you go back to the paragraph above where I summarize the action, you will notice that it sounds nothing like a stage play. Narrated from the camera's (the spectator's) point of view, what we are watching is not a theatre piece but a cinematic sequence; even just to read the summary, you are almost forced to imaginatively supply screen transitions and camera effects. Take away the neat narrative progression provided by the tracking shot and we really have no idea what Dick and Jane are up to. Mixed media, in this case, invites complicity, not collaboration. After mocking the rival directors for inanely contending over whose medium is closer to the 'real', we find ourselves caught up in a mixed-media situation where our own mediated experience of the 'real' is a ruse to content us with the suppressed and the strange. We escape from art-speak, only to fall into the trap of the unspoken.

In *At Home With Dick and Jane*, theatre and the digital come together without ever really addressing each other directly. As I see it, nothing could be more 'digital'. It is not any single technological innovation – computers, digital recording, the Internet – that we typically mean when we invoke the digital. Instead, we tend to have in our minds a much more diffuse expectation and experience of technologically motivated cultural change. 'The tension between immediate and mediated' is a perfect example of this kind of ambient broad-stroke concern, and it is what the Electric Company Theatre claim as their 'source of inspiration' for *At Home With Dick and Jane*. They find that unresolved tension in the problem of an expanding media platform for artspeak; in the primacy claims of theatre over film, and vice versa; in the perils and pleasures of mixed media; in the fine line between narcissism and over-specialization, and between intimate knowledge and customization; and in the idea of the 'real' as a product of the mediated. In exploring these tensions, *At Home With Dick and Jane* builds on its own use of multimedia performance, digital content, audience participation, site-specific theatre, and a blurring of the lines between playwright, director, players, spectators, stage designers, dramaturg, and technologist. Treating *At Home With Dick and Jane*, a theatre work that turns on the relationship between theatre and the digital, at some length allows us to get entangled in the uncertain artistic constraints, aesthetic forms, and theoretical underpinnings of these various performance elements and themes. The other examples discussed in this book will make their interest in the digital more explicit, often giving the impression that digital theatre is itself an established field. But as *At Home With Dick and Jane* means to remind us, much of what we are likely to consider new or threatening or promising about digitally mediated theatre is, to borrow a phrase from the media historian Lisa Gitelman, 'always already in play' on the side of 'live' theatre as well (*Always Already New: Media, History, and the Data of Culture*, 2006, p. xii). A simple optimism in the 'very human' quality (a favourite phrase of the belittled theatre director) of live theatre fails to account for the mediated nature of that assumed specialness, or the fact that the same set of concerns that have become a peg for the anti-digital – intrusiveness, loss of agency, loopy pointlessness, mere connectivity in place of genuine relationality – can attach to the ideally human as well.

Online presence

Now, in addition to laying out an excellent meditative labyrinth on these issues, *At Home With Dick and Jane* sets a wide-ranging practical example of the pairing of theatre and the digital. Despite the work's implicit critique of expanding digital media platforms, the Electric Company Theatre is not at all averse to taking full advantage of those platforms itself. I have already noted the performance site: the Centre for Digital Media, as part of the HIVE 3 theatre festival put on by the Progress Lab in 2010 (an earlier version of *At Home With Dick and Jane* was staged in 2006 at the Chapel Arts centre as part of the first HIVE festival). Given the context of its production, the manner in which the mock interview draws special attention to itself as a digital video, both in its style and in its format, takes on further significance. Likewise, it is unsurprising to later discover the video posted on YouTube; in fact, as soon as you think about it, the extension of the work onto YouTube is implied throughout – by the issue of digital-born content and universal audiences, but perhaps even more so by the whole theme of Dick and Jane's social art making and their homemade video production (the one we participate in as camera operator).

As of this writing, you can view the video of the mock interview for yourself at www.youtube.com/watch?v=EMdWULDLomw. You can also take a behind-the-scenes look at the behind-the-camera experience of the live performance at www.youtube.com/watch?v=cDoz38xD-dM. Or, to add an entirely new layer of complication to the work, you can watch a digital film version of the 'live' performance at www.youtube.com/watch?v=IsCX3MhyndA. (Alternatively, the video version and backstage POV can be viewed on the Electric Company Theatre's website at electriccompanytheatre.com/video-online/.)

One consequence of extending the work onto YouTube is that 'real' viewers have the ability to post comments. In response to the digital film of Dick and Jane at home, for instance: 'This is really really so adorable:D (Martina Vel'ká)' and 'that's so cute <3 (Finn Storm)'. In response to the mock interview: 'How can they keep a straight face!!!!! *strangled giggles* (EwigeStudentin)' and 'a perfect spoof

on director/writer interviews. Well done! (L Champlin)';
also, 'wish I lived in canada, love from New Zealand!
(Luellavoir)' and 'the way jonathan says the word "talking"… he is canadian right? (iDJMIXTRESS)'. Presumably
unintended, or at least unplanned, the comments posted
on YouTube by viewers further exemplify how the digital
brings about a certain kind of discourse about the arts.
Mainly, the comments keep within the realm of the affir-
mational and the mundane. As mere proofs of the com-
menters' proper response, they are another instance of
complicity, rather than genuine collaboration or contribu-
tion (or criticism). Somewhat more unusual are the comments that veer towards the random, such as the statement
about desiring to live in Canada or the observation about
Jonathan's Canadian accent (Jonathan Young is the actor
who plays the theatre director, as well as the role of Dick;
Young is also a co-artistic director of the Electric Company
Theatre, along with Kim Collier, who plays the film director and Jane). In contrast to the overly serious art-speak of
the mock interviewees and the overly adorable art-making
affection of Dick and Jane at home, the YouTube comments –
although altogether in keeping with the genre of YouTube
commenting – have the problem of being overly trite or off
topic.

At the level of online interconnectivity, dealing in generalities, whether of a positive, negative, or oblique sort,
is of course fully expected. But insofar as we might perceive something inherently performative about this cycle
of YouTube video posting and viewer commenting, deeper

questions about the nature of art making and art response again come to the fore. The novelist and performance studies scholar Barbara Browning has written a novel, *I'm Trying to Reach You* (2011), about the mysterious relationships – to art, to other personas online, to your own online persona – that compulsive YouTube viewing (liking, lurking, interloping) can produce. The novel's narrator, Gray Adams, is a performance studies academic who turns his YouTube procrastination habit into a scholarly investigation. Performativity and voyeurism in the digital sphere, Adams discovers, lends itself to a discursive scape of the 'overheard and understated' (p. 163). Desire for interconnectivity exposes the fundamental ambiguousness of our attempts to build expressive relationships, online or off; we each, as Adams explains it, have 'something to find, something to hide, or something [we] desperately want to show' (p. 164). A pervasive sense of falseness is present in such a culture, as we attempt to 'maintain the fiction of non-theatricality, of non-spectacularity, of the extreme understatement of the performance' (p. 163). And yet the underlying principle of relationship building still seems to hold out a path for more positive and constructive exchange. The mock interviewees lack this willingness to build relationships. The happy fiction of Dick and Jane's companionate collaboration is precisely maintained through 'extreme understatement', which could be a good thing, a bad thing, neither or both. Likewise, whatever might be lacking in terms of a meaningful relationship between YouTube video makers and online audiences, the practical (and political) potential of that relationship building could go either way, and so the point is to put oneself to the test in order to let cultural dynamics decide.

Which brings us back to where we started with the Electric Company Theatre – not their artistic work, but their mission statement, with its remarkable claims about, for instance, working 'to reach across cultures, backgrounds, economics, and ideology to find the universal elements that connect all members of our community'. How to square *At Home With Dick and Jane*'s critique of art-speak and over-stated purposefulness with the company's own extraordinary assertions of theatre-cultural ambition? The Electric Company's vision has high idealistic motives, but practical application would seem to give the lie to it. Extending their site-specific theatre work into a YouTube video series, for example, fulfils the company's goal of 'creating productions that go beyond the confines of the traditional stage' (all quotes taken from electriccompanytheatre.com/company/mission-history/). But the actual audience of the YouTube videos fails to suggest any profound changes in the reach of their work. Even if the 500 to 1,000 viewers of each video are considered a relatively substantial number, the evidence of their comments suggests that only a familiar, existing audience has been reached – people who know Jonathan, for instance, or who want to be encouraging. Democratic access and arts provocation are very different goals. A strong cultural belief in 'universal' outreach and connectivity through the arts sits oddly beside such YouTube comments as the one by 'Luellavoir' about being from New Zealand but thinking Canada would be a great place to live (because better theatre is produced there? Regardless, how could this mockumentary video possibly elicit such a response on its own?). When we evaluate these responses against the Electric Company's self-declared standard of a 'theatre that is life affirming, inspiring, and provocative', we are left to find an audience that is no more than warmly amused, gigglish, and cryptically interested in Canada.

The point is not that the digital is incapable of rewarding our lofty cultural beliefs. It is rather that the theatre has begun to explore – self-awarely, in the case of the Electric Company Theatre – the social and theoretical underpinnings of artistic exchange and cultural work, and has discovered a traffic flow problem at the intersection. Despite the practical doubtfulness of the Electric Company's statements of entrepreneurial purposefulness, their artistic work is uniquely alert to the nature of that doubtfulness, especially as exposed by the digital. For instance, the YouTube experiment is meant to be analytical as well as hopeful: in expanding outside 'the confines of the traditional stage', the Electric Company is looking to devise projects in which, in their words, 'the theatre itself is given a metaphoric presence and the role of the audience (the act of watching) becomes thematic content'. The questions we have been asking about theatre and the digital are certainly not incidental to *At Home With Dick and Jane*, although perhaps they are not entirely intended, either: it is a work of theatre that is interested in itself as a work of theatre in relation to other social and media variables of interconnectivity and intersubjectivity, so that what results, to use a phrase from the anthropologist George Stocking, is 'an experiment in multiple contextualization' (*Victorian Anthropology*, 1987, p. xii). Whereas the loopy self-referentiality of the mock interviewees shows up the ill-conceived conceit of art that is too much interested in itself, the Electric Company avoids narcissism in favour of empiricism. Mixed media and 'multiple contextualization' not only challenge the conventions of theatre; they also open the way for real alternatives, at the level of both conception and habit. 'With each project we strive to build from what we know', the company explains, 'and to abandon it.' Experiment leads to disavowal, and progress stems directly from this sense of conflict, of feeling stopped.

On the theoretical side, pushing at the digital frontier means rethinking the very idea of theatre and the nature and status of the audience. On the more practical, entrepreneurial side, the digital embrace is about building relationships. The question of how the two sides mutually support each other will have to wait until the final section of this book. For now, let me just note the many ways in which relationship building is crucial to the logic of the Electric Company's theatre-cultural mission. I have already mentioned their ambition to 'connect all members of our community' by cultivating a universal, common ground; the target here is a larger audience, of course, but also a more inclusive one, integrated and bolstered by meaningfully shared concerns. Additionally, their hopeful ideal is not only to connect with a wider audience, but to engage more fully with the 'community' – an image of the theatre arts as socially relevant and actively responsive, rather than autonomous and proscriptive. To deliver on that promise, the company seeks out 'partnerships with community organizations, businesses, government, schools and individuals'. Those partnerships are made possible (they say) because of their commitments to finding common ground; another reason is their 'common respect' for different forms and styles, as well as their explorative interest in 'new technology', allowing them to see potential for creativity and artistic purpose on almost any front. That openness to multimodal innovation also underlies their sense of being 'highly collaborative', with the artisanal objective of creating 'a constructive and rewarding environment for artists, encouraging each member of a given project to think outside their traditional roles in the process of making a play'. Finally, although the company believes itself to be an 'innovator in multimedia performance, we remain firm believers in the importance of live theatre to promote community interaction in the age of YouTube'. Live interaction — live theatre — is the entailment between the online extension of their projects and their community outreach goals. A whole set of values and beliefs related to access, organization, collaboration, communication, connectivity, intersubjectivity, integration, extension, and innovation are shuttling back and forth here between the company's theatre-cultural optimism and their sense of digital opportunism. *At Home With Dick and Jane* is about the limitations of exactly this sort of optimism when it comes to the question of mediated arts production. And yet: the Electric Company Theatre still aims to achieve through cultural work that which their artistic work denies. This paradox between theatrical creativity that is theoretically self-aware and theatrical entrepreneurialism that is wilfully self-believing is, as we will continue to see, at the crux of the argument for whole-scale progress in the arts.

What can theatre do without?

The next two examples involve performances – the Elevator Repair Service's *Shuffle* (New York Public Library/FuturePerfect, New York, 2010) and Neworld Theatre's PodPlays project (PuSh International, Vancouver, 2011) – that seek to achieve through negation what *At Home With Dick and Jane* attempts through mixed comparison. *Shuffle* is a theatre project that employs the digital to get around the need for a playwright or even a play; PodPlays is a theatre project that makes use of the digital to do away with the space of the theatre and the need for performers. Plays, playwrights, directors, theatres, performers, liveness – if these can be done without, what, if anything, are we left with at the core of the theatre? Again, we will hear claims about experimentation and progress. The idea that the digital might somehow reveal to us the limit case of the theatre is, for a number of reasons, useful for the purpose of predicting a different future, one that has the potential to reinvent the theatre, to reclaim its purpose, and to reconstruct the whole of its cultural project. Grand rhetoric and digital arts experimentation are very much on the same frequency and wavelength. The way forward from there is still to be determined.

The Elevator Repair Service (ERS) appear to have been consciously influenced by these considerations in their production of *Shuffle*: how to balance radically innovative creative procedures with coherent artistic purpose? Unlike the Electric Company, however, ERS show little concern for coherence as a problem of audience or theatre-cultural purposefulness. Coherence, instead, represents an aesthetic curiosity, something to fetishistically pry into. This fetishistic aspect is a unique factor in the case of *Shuffle*: what almost certainly would have been dismissed as a trivial or literary indulgence without the presence of the digital becomes an 'intermittently lovely' (*New York Times*) or 'cool' (*New Yorker*) performance work because of the group's collaboration with the digital.

To explain *Shuffle*, it is helpful to break the performance down into its parts. First, the setting: the periodical room at the main building of the New York Public Library (the actual building, that is to say, not a set design). The large room is divided into nine stations, such as the desk behind the checkout counter or a library table near to the photocopier. The setting determines the action: actors can move from one station to another at any time, as prompted by the script; each station correlates with a particular mode of action, such as holding a champagne flute while delivering one's lines (at the desk behind the checkout counter) or rapidly picking up and putting down one of three paperback novels (at the library table near the photocopier). The focus, however, is less on the action than on the words, partly because we are in a library, where words have a certain

38

expected quality of meaning, but also partly because the words, digitally projected onto the wall, are conspicuously apparent to the audience. But that is the least of what puts the words at the centre of our attention: the words themselves are conspicuous, both in their recognizable original state and in the newly unrecognizable forms generated out of the originals. Originally, the words come from a trio of American novels: William Faulkner's *The Sound and the Fury* (1929), F. Scott Fitzgerald's *The Great Gatsby* (1925), and Ernest Hemingway's *The Sun Also Rises* (1926). In addition to the copious paperback editions scattered about the library room and carried around by the actors, the novels exist as digital text files in a computer database. Applying a diverse set of software and statistical algorithms, the computer constantly searches and retrieves from that database, creating a mash-up of the three novels in paired strings of dialogue, contrasting lines, seemingly random paragraphs, and so on. It is through this method of digital text processing that the script for each actor is generated in real time during an ongoing performance. The same words that are projected on the wall for the audience are delivered, in synch, to iPods visibly hidden in the paperback books that each actor carries with them. Reading the lines – sometimes alone, sometimes in dialogue, sometimes simultaneously (cacophonously) – happens at a mostly frantic pace, with the actors quickly moving between stations as prompted while trying to keep up with the text feed. The audience is free to roam and mingle. The hope is to find some snippets of sense, either familiar – the self-assuring pleasure of hearing a passage that you recognize as belonging, in part or in full, to one of the novels – or newly created – the fortuitous delight in coming across a combination of passages, out of sequence and out of context, but for whatever reason making sense together. Or, potentially, the frequent awkwardness and confusion could be said to have an aesthetic of its own.

Not having any idea of how the material we are presented with has been pre-sorted and arranged by algorithms is typical of the way we experience digital information online (Google is notoriously secretive about its search algorithms), so there is that implicit moral to be drawn from *Shuffle*. But the ongoing disarticulation and reconfiguring of the familiar novels, according to the director, John Collins, should not leave us thinking about the negative effects of treating meaningful information as data. The idea is that they are 'playing with the text', taking an outlook of productive ambivalence on the problem of making sense (quoted in Samantha Henig, 'Hemingway, Faulkner, and Fitzgerald: The Remix', 2011). Wanting to scrutinize the source assumes that meaning results from intention. But the playful spirit of *Shuffle*, like the practice of online information seeking, takes wilful discovery as its principle instead: meaning should not be scrutinized but observed, and then recombined and reinvented again, perhaps endlessly and always with complete open-mindedness. Michael Nielsen, a quantum-computing scientist who has become an advocate for new methods of collaborative science, argues that such experiments in 'the way discoveries are made are more important than any single discovery'

(*Reinventing Discovery: The New Era of Discovery*, 2011, p. 3). *Shuffle* is precisely intended as this kind of experiment, putting process ahead of any definite purpose. 'Audience members derived pleasure from the possibility of discovering new relationships and alternative insights,' according to Wayne Ashley, one of the many artistic collaborators on the project (quoted in a blog interview with Digitalarti, 'FuturePerfect in New York', 2012, www. digitalarti.com/blog/digitalarti_mag/futureperfect_in_ new_york). Discovery is a pleasure, an instinctual sense; it results from chance and circumstance, randomness and collaboration, rather than method or even focus. In a way, what is at stake is an aesthetic sensibility, one that finds meaning, not distraction, in data flows and playful experiments of unlikely combinations.

To argue, as both Nielsen and Ashley do, that playfully trying out new modes of discovery is more important than any actual discoveries that result does not accord with our usual notions of progress. For Ashley, promoting this conceptual shift – from the idea of progress as special achievement to progress as routine practice – provides the foundational mission of his New York-based performance and technology production company, FuturePerfect (which commissioned and collaborated with ERS on *Shuffle*). In direct contrast to the Electric Company Theatre's coherent and optimistic ambitions, FuturePerfect, despite the company's name, wants theatre artists to resist looking positively towards the future: 'The name FuturePerfect refers to the future perfect tense', Ashley explains, 'and not to a utopian future made better by technology or art' (all quotes from the blog interview with Digitalarti). The twinned seduction of easy optimism and grand rhetoric is exactly what needs to be dispelled, or at least mitigated: 'The name is a way of complicating the relationship of past, present and future — with no predictable outcome, and possibility for ambiguity, circularity, and no finality.' Because we tend to see in digital technology an already outlined promise of the future, Ashley reasons, we become encouraged in the belief that that future can somehow be systematically worked towards. Misled by such false assurances, too many works of digital theatre end up buying into the hype of the 'new', the 'better', and the 'predictable'. Ashley argues that to get around the faddishness and commercialization that those works are prone to, what we need is a certain kind of collaboration, and more of it:

> [I am] invested in a kind of productive messiness that emerges because artists and scientists together are exploring, thinking, and making across different practices and ideas previously unavailable to one another. ... I am driven by an almost compulsive desire to bring people together who seem to occupy disparate histories, training systems, cultural backgrounds, and disciplinary fields. My experience is that this kind of deep heterogeneous play has the potential of producing new questions and insights into both artistic and social processes. Collaborators are, by necessity,

forced to re-think habitual ways of working and knowing. ('FuturePerfect in New York')

Although the Electric Company Theatre similarly emphasizes collaboration as part of their mission, the rhetoric here is remarkably different. 'Universal elements', 'common respect', and a 'constructive and rewarding environment' all fall under the mantle of collaboration for the Electric Company. Alternatively, FuturePerfect builds their case for collaboration around key values of 'messiness', 'difference', 'disparity', 'heterogeneity', and 'forced' uneasiness and interrogativeness. Against the companionate security of shared purpose and mutual effort, Ashley prefers the productive threat that goes with pairing together confused and competing factions, left to their uncertainty. *Shuffle* is a perfect example of this method of collaborative mismatching: library staff and patrons mix with theatre performers; a media artist (Ben Rubin), a statistician (Mark Hansen), and a theatre director (John Collins) share creative control, along with a computer program that works on its own; and the whole project, of course, involves turning novels into play scripts, repurposing literary texts as informational data, and devolving narrative storytelling into random utterance.

To be sure, the Electric Company and FuturePerfect, in the final account, actually share most of the same values, even if their rhetoric differs. 'FuturePerfect chooses artists', Ashley goes on to explain, 'whose works make possible dialogues between seemingly impenetrable institutions, forms of knowledge, classes, and ethnicities.' Finding common ground, whether at the exposed level of ideology or the expressed level of values, produces a greater consciousness of both the aesthetic and the cultural terms of artistic production. By making the unfamiliar routine – that is, not making the unfamiliar familiar, but making unfamiliarity something we are more used to being confronted by, and therefore more open to – we gain a certain degree of control over the unpredictable and contested situation of the present, in anticipation, rather than assertion, of the future. ERS/FuturePerfect's *Shuffle*, like Electric Company's *At Home With Dick and Jane*, is a digital theatre project in which cooperative practices of artistic production, the larger mission of theatre entrepreneurialism, and the actual content and ideas of the work all come together around the same logic. Is that multi-purpose logic the manifestation of the digital? Can it culminate in anything other than itself?

Theatre apps

Neworld Theatre's PodPlays project is an example of a digital theatre application. An application in the sense of 'applied theatre', which theatre professor Judith Ackroyd defines as any theatre work which shares 'a belief in the power of the theatre form to address something beyond the form itself' ('Applied Theatre: Problems and Possibilities', 2000; quoted in Helen Nicholson, *Applied Drama: The Gift of Theatre*, 2005, p. 3). The PodPlays are also applications in the digital sense, insofar as they are packaged and sold as iPod apps.

The incisiveness of theatre outreach can often resemble commercialism. Aside from the good intentions, the goal of making new and useful theatre that appeals to non-theatre-going audiences is, by definition, a type of publicity cause. On the one hand, there is reason to believe in the democratic ambitions of releasing theatre from its at-the-theatre rituals, moving the theatre to the masses. Walter Benjamin, reflecting on the age of mechanical reproduction eighty years ago, expressed a cautious optimism about the potential for freeing art and cultural participation from its formal, material, and institutional rootedness. Publicity, from a liberatory outlook of this sort, is about making public theatre open to all, and making it accessible, not just available.

On the other hand, as the cultural anthropologist Greg Urban argues in *Metaculture: How Culture Moves through the World* (2001), such hopes for broadening circulation are also 'at the heart of the expansion of capital' (p. xiv). Accessibility is not sufficient; promising new platforms for cultural outreach ultimately depend on creating a demand for the works they produce. But not just the works, which is where Urban's notion of 'metaculture' comes in: creating interest in the actual works is only one kind of 'demand structure'. Another kind is the demand for having something to talk about, which newspapers, journals, magazines, and blogs rely on to attract audiences of their own. The culture industry, according to Urban, depends as much on an economy of discussion between theatre makers and reviewers as it does on an economy of exchange between theatre makers and audiences. Promising new works, even without reaching actual theatregoers, have special value because they are great for keeping up a discourse about newness. The market for commentary and reviews revolves around the production and discussion of a constantly renewed sense of the new. Urban's word for this is 'metaculture': the strand of our culture that supplies 'newness' to cultural objects by talking about them in relation to other interesting social phenomena and cultural trends. What is produced is interest, both in the talk itself and in the object being talked about. 'In order for [a] review to circulate,' Urban writes, 'it must be seen as an interesting response':

> By attracting more readers, a successful review will increase its own circulation; it will also impart that interest to the [cultural object], thereby increasing demand for it. In this case, culture and metaculture end up reinforcing each other's circulatory potential. ... The culture of modernity depends upon the creation of social institutions organized around a metaculture of newness that directly contribute to the expansion of capitalism and democratic discourse. (p. xiv)

The more interesting a work is made to seem in its newness, the more likely it is to enter into circulation. That circulation can result in actual commercial and cultural activity, such as theatregoing. But sometimes it is enough just to be talked about: under certain conditions, and especially in our age of blogging and posting and tweeting, metaculture can sometimes end up happily circulating on its own, without ever leading to much or any cultural activity on the ground.

All this helps us to address a fact that is hard to ignore when discussing digital theatre projects: the exuberance for their newness is often more interesting to talk about than to actually experience. Podplays could fall into this category (as could Twitter plays – 'trendy and trivial' in their current form, John Muse concludes in his article on '140 Characters in Search of a Theater' in the journal *Theater*).

If you go to the webpage of The Wireless Theatre Company (which is the only place you can 'go' to their theatre; wirelesstheatrecompany.co.uk), you might be surprised by the whole-scale impression given of Internet audio drama as an already established cultural industry. There appear to be at least two official publications dedicated to the form, *Audio Drama Review* and *EarStory Review*; multiple award-giving organizations that recognize the category of 'online/multiplatform dramas', including The Radio Academy and the Silver Ogle Awards; numerous blogs, such as the Audio Drama Blog and Radio Drama Revival; and, of course, a host of competitors. Additionally, a celebrity endorsement from the actor Jude Law confirms, 'What a fantastic idea Wireless Theatre is!' Far from being an entirely new form of theatre, podplays are made to seem already fully integrated into our cultural field, born full-blown with what Urban would describe as their own 'pathways and networks of circulation' (*Metaculture*, p. 178).

The impression of established cultural activity and the impression of newness are related in this case. First, there is the fact that, like all new forms, podplays are not really new at all. Radio dramas, as I mentioned at the beginning of this book, were once thought to hold such obvious artistic and commercial potential that many theatre people thought they would inevitably make live performance obsolete. The playwright and theatre theorist Bertolt Brecht, for one, was enthralled by the prospect, imagining a future in which radio might become a multi-directional 'apparatus for distribution' and thereby become 'the finest possible communication apparatus in public life, a vast network of pipes' (quoted in David Saltz, 'Performing Arts', 2004, p. 128). Brecht's idea was that the public, equipped with the technological means, might be led to create and circulate their own citizen forms of theatre. Digital networks of course entail such possibilities, and clearly amateur theatre making – or at least the dissemination of such theatre making – is thriving like never before. The Wireless Theatre Company, in this light, welcomes listener submissions, offering (for a fee) their professional recording services for producing digitally formatted voice-reels of your own play scripts. Of course, podplays are easy enough to produce on your home computer as well. Indeed, when mention is made of competitors, those competitors appear to be mainly Internet audio drama hobbyists and theatre artists working on their own. The difference between professional and amateur might come down to the quality of production (*EarStory Review* cites The Wireless Theatre Company's 'professional' production in determining that they are 'the best internet audio drama production company' out there right now), or the factor of monetization (although The Wireless Theatre Company offers all their podplays for free, they place audio advertisements on the download). Regardless, it is more important what professionals and amateurs share: the same sustaining demand structure – the same 'excitement', as The Wireless Theatre Company refers to it.

So far, that excitement is not primarily on the side of audience interest, which appears to be low even in comparison to live theatre attendance (and, somewhat strangely, unconnected with the market for audio books). Instead, what appears to be giving energy and purpose to the enterprise is the creators' and reviewers' own sense of its newness. The Listener's Feedback page on The Wireless Theatre Company website is filled with platitudes of newness: 'pioneering spirit of innovation' (The Radio Academy), 'new and exciting' (John Park, editor of *Fringe Report*), 'a breath of fresh air' (Ronald Lacey, listener). Taken altogether, what we are seeing is an example of what Urban terms a 'metacultural' phenomenon: a self-reflexive culture that, by virtue of its participants laying claim to newness, creates a self-sufficient interest in itself. Exchange of cultural objects between makers and audiences is still the underlying goal, but not a determining one. Promises of newness among makers and reviewers can function perfectly well as a 'pathway and network of circulation' without any substantial audience interest whatsoever.

The coterie publicity blurbs that The Wireless Theatre Company posts on their webpage operate in much the same way as the theatre mission statements that are posted on the Electric Company Theatre's and FuturePerfect's webpages. But whereas The Wireless Theatre Company participates in a metacultural network of actors, bloggers, and hobbyists, the Electric Company Theatre and FuturePerfect are looking to connect with a very different network of reviewers – theatre grants committees, corporate and community sponsors, private patrons, and festival organizers, all of whom have been silently omitted from our discussion about theatre and the digital so far. For most theatre companies, especially experimental ones, bridging the demand structure of funding and support is a more pressing and practical need than putting actual audiences in seats.

Mission statements are a form of discursive mediation essential to grants applications and funding requests. Because of the Internet, theatre mission statements have become public-facing documents as well, and therefore serve publicity ends of their own. But even so, the public is unlikely to ever see a theatre company's mission statement, and would almost never think to pay close attention to one. Which is for the best, as mission statements are rarely written to withstand critical scrutiny. As we have already seen, a discourse of generalities is typical of mission statements – a distinctive blend of cultural optimism, entrepreneurial self-belief, collaborative spirit, and an interest in new forms. A metaculture of broadening artistic and cultural objectives – newness, but specifically an agenda-driven newness — has developed in line with the 'pathways and networks' of funding and support that sustain much of our contemporary theatre arts scene. For those who make theatre or who have served on a grants council or cultural development board in our digital age, the pairing of theatre and the digital is a quite obvious fit: the digital provides a seemingly direct means of contributing 'to the expansion of capitalism and democratic discourse', which Urban sees as the overall mission (for better or worse) of modern culture. The 'excitement' of arts innovation lies in the purposefulness of cultural expansion. Expanding into the realm of the digital has, accordingly, stirred much excitement.

Podplays are a great example of a digital theatre form that has more value, or at least more utility, as an externally funded public arts project than a commercially oriented one. The digital factor that adds particular excitement to podplays, besides the affordances of online downloads and computer recording software, is the 'pod' factor: the audio dramas can be listened to on a portable media player, such as an iPod, while the listener wanders around a specific site. Politically motivated theatre artists have been quick to realize the inherent potential for cultural intervention.

Neworld Theatre specializes, according to their mission statement, in 'non-didactic, politically-engaged productions' (www.neworldtheatre.com/company-history. html). Balancing the goals of 'non-didactic' and 'politically-engaged', for them, is achieved through open collaboration with community partners, a focus on local issues, an appreciation of popular forms, and the creative use of multimedia

technologies. In a curatorial statement written to promote the inclusion of Neworld Theatre's PodPlays as part
of the 2010 PuSh International Performing Arts Festival
in Vancouver, the festival's associate curator, Dani Fecko,
puts herself forward as an example of someone positively
affected by their work:

> In a time of iPods and cell phones, I will admit
> I am not usually as open to taking in my sur-
> roundings as I should be. I'm not proud of this. ...
> Ironically, experiencing Neworld Theatre's
> PodPlays changed everything for me. PodPlays
> allowed me to see Vancouver in a brand new
> light. It allowed me to look up. I was no longer
> in 'the City of Glass', but in a city drenched with
> architecture, urban landscaping, and history. I
> was in a city with a story. More to the point,
> I was in a city whose people had stories. ... It
> left me in quiet reflection about how I fit into
> the intricacies of a seemingly young city, which
> has taken the lives of so many to create. I was
> uplifted about the creativity of my peers and
> so proud to be a part of a community that so
> deeply cares about its background. ('PodPlays –
> Curatorial Statement', 2010, pushfestival.ca/
> 2014/12/podplays-curatorial-statement/)

Fecko's self-account begins by acknowledging a personal
problem, which turns on a civic concern: her personal
media use in public spaces was making her less publicly

aware. Neworld Theatre's PodPlays presented a meaningful solution, all the more effective because it met her on her own ground: instead of critiquing the problem of personal media use, they engage the problem directly, changing the nature of use through creative reorientation. Unlike radio dramas, Neworld Theatre's PodPlays are theatrical in the sense of emphasizing the non-verbal – the space of the city, its architecture, and its people – as well as the verbal – the telling of a story. 'Reflection' is claimed as a valued outcome, but it is a uniquely active mode of reflection. The theatrical performance is at once both a mental drama and an environmental one: the city, literally, becomes the stage; it is also the setting, as well as an attention-grabbing performer. What initially stands as the problem, a lack of civic attentiveness, comes to be experienced as a theatrical pleasure. According to Fecko's account, cultural participation – listening to one of Neworld Theatre's PodPlays – is not an end in itself, but a potent agent of social change, instilling civic pride and sociable self-awareness by providing an immersive theatrical experience. Cultural engagement and theatre production are in sync. Freeing up the theatre so that it can be carried around by the people allows for the possibility that the people might be carried along by the theatre on the way to becoming better public selves.

These are grand claims again, but, in this case, the logic of Neworld Theatre's PodPlays project comes with a certain degree of reasonableness, and humaneness. The theatrical work is not immersed in itself, as too many digital theatre projects often end up seeming. The best examples (some of

Neworld Theatre's PodPlays, admittedly, are less successful than others) give the opposite feeling of scale: the city
around us looms large with interest as the podplay devolves
into a half-told story, experienced more like a memory than
a dramatic performance. 'Look Up', a 2011 podplay written and performed by Neworld Theatre's Adrienne Wong,
achieves this effect through the story of a lover trying to
gather her thoughts about why we have drifted apart. The
mutuality of the story, the sense that we are following her
directions (which we are actually intended to follow: a map
and directions can be found online at www.neworldtheatre.
com/productions-podplays.html) around the city not as an
outsider, but as someone who has shared in the life memo-
ries being recalled, makes for an odd but memorable experience. It is as if we have cast ourselves in the play as well,
or as if in agreeing to follow her directions, we somehow
(when it works) begin to feel like we have just shared something. The story elements are slight – a decision to move
out West, downsizing to an apartment with a view, shoe
shopping, recollections of different kinds of rain – but that
seems to be the point. Easily, the audio play can fade into the
background, prompting your own thoughts, or leading you
to focus on the wrong thing, and then leading you to over-
focus as you try to figure out what particular building or
mountain crest or sidewalk planter she is actually referring
to. The ideas and the story do not demand much attention,
but the meaning accrues much more in the environmental
connections than in anything verbal or analytical. Whether
any of that ultimately encourages a bettering of oneself is

another question. The more likely result is that it lends you an additional perspective on the city that is not your own, which depending on how you relate to your city, could end up influencing a lot about yourself. (A first-person video experience of 'Look Up' is online at Neworld Theatre's website: www.neworldtheatre.com/video.html.)

It is easy to see why a city arts council or community engagement programme would want to fund such a project. Other, similar audio walks projects have been developed as forms of tourism – such as the UK's Soundmap Audio Tours and Footnotes Audio Walks – or as high-concept advertising – New York-based Soundwalk has had works commissioned by fashion design firms such as Chanel, Nina Ricci, and Louis Vuitton, though it also produces more purely artistic works, devised for 'poetic discovery of a city, on the bridge between Baudelarian stroll and cinematic experience' (see Soundwalk's mission statement at www.soundwalk.com/#/ABOUT/). Another Canadian artist, Janet Cardiff, has collaborated on a series of audio walks on the higher side of concept as well, but these have been funded as public arts projects, with works commissioned by the Culture Department of the City of Jena, Germany ('Memory Field', 2006), Arts Council England ('The Missing Voice (Case Study B)', 1999), and New York City's Public Art Fund ('Her Long Black Hair', 2004). Likewise, Neworld Theatre's PodPlays have been variously supported by public arts funding, including awards from the Canada Council for the Arts, the British Columbia Arts Council, and the Vancouver Foundation, and by corporate community investment funds, such as the Vancouver Sun Innovation Awards and the TELUS Vancouver Community Board. The PodPlays project has become an ever broadening cultural-engagement platform for Neworld Theatre. In addition to the podplays they created for the PuSh International Performing Arts Festival, they have produced a series, 'PodPlays 125', with support from the City of Vancouver's 125th Anniversary Grants Program and the Government of Canada, and a standalone work, 'The Oppenheimer Incident', as part of the 2010 Powell Street Festival to inaugurate the newly renovated Oppenheimer Park in the Downtown Eastside of Vancouver. In 2014, in collaboration with the Inclusive Design Research Centre and the Roundhouse Community Centre, they planned a 'City Kids Play Lab' for the Vancouver International Children's Festival, a 'multi-media theatre project about city living and civic responsibility sourced from kids' experiences, stories, and artwork', which they refer to as 'an evolution of Neworld Theatre's popular workshop and production series' (www.neworldtheatre.com/productions-me-on-the-map.html).

Their notion of 'evolution' is revealing. This is not the type of theatre project that aspires to the status of a unique work of 'striking and ingenious invention' (Artaud). As opposed to narrowing their artistic focus to produce a singular cultural work, Neworld Theatre seeks to 'evolve' (their word, or 'expand', to use Urban's word) their metacultural purpose in widening, overlapping circles of public arts initiatives and political engagement. Given how a metacultural discourse of cultural engagement works – setting shared goals and values, pointing up mutual benefits and positive gains – the pursuit of 'unpredictable insight' (Nelson) needs to be turned around as well: instead of conceding unpredictability, Neworld Theatre strives for reasonableness in their planning and accessibility in their design. At stake is funding, but also public purpose.

Neworld Theatre's PodPlays project, in all these ways, is a type of solution-oriented theatre. They begin by observing two problems: the typical didacticism of politically engaged theatre, and the public distraction of personal media use – the problem with the former is that it leads to a lack of interest; the latter, too much interest. Solution: the theatre is reformulated as a form of pleasurable distraction, which gets around the problem of didacticism. Conversely, personal media use is repurposed as a mode of theatrical spectatorship, which gets around the problem of distraction. The reasonableness of Neworld Theatre's PodPlays project can be questioned at the level of actuality (I have my doubts about social and cultural engagement as currently practised by most theatre makers, and about the quality of such works as interesting theatre), but the logical, rhetorical angle is undeniable. Artistically, theatre and the digital might still be feeling each other out, but metaculturally they are already in the midst of a 'slow-burning love affair' – the characterization of theatre and the digital made by The Mission Business, the Toronto-based theatre company behind the next (and last) performance example.

Mission business

The contemporary American theatre avant-gardist Richard Foreman is a believer in the philosophical capacity of the theatre to produce forceful insight, but he is also a realist. During rehearsals, Foreman claims to tell performers to 'be hostile toward the audience. Don't make them love you':

> Always believe that when you have a line, you are saying the most intelligent thing in the world but that only a few people in the audience are going to get it. You should play the show only for those few. ... It is as if each of your lines held overwhelming information in coded form. And the audience, save for a few, are vulgar hooligans to whom you have no desire to present your wonderful ideas. (*Unbalancing Acts: Foundations for a Theatre*, 1993, 42–43)

As Foreman sees it, disengaging with the audience at the general level is a precondition for engaging the insightful individual on a one-to-one basis. The theatrical event is not a group activity, but a test of the selfless individual's will and intelligence. Whereas the popular theatregoer might be looking for a sociable outing and a good time, 'total theatre' (Foreman's term) imposes an unsettling trial of philosophical exchange. The nature of that exchange is non-negotiable and one-directional: the theatre artists have possession of 'wonderful ideas', and their task is to deliver that 'overwhelming information', with aggression and indignation, to the chosen few.

Forceful, shock-and-awe strategies of theatrical engagement are neither reasonable nor humane, nor are they meant to be. A 'theatre of cruelty', to use Artaud's terminology, is about prying away at the social instability of insight and exposing problems of miscommunication, not treating those problems as correctable. To a 'politically engaged' theatre maker looking for practical solutions to cultural and theatrical problems, the idea that art's truths might, needfully, be difficult to access, contradictory, and without any lasting power would seem to undermine the whole project and cause of cultural intervention through theatre.

We have not seen that. That is, we have not seen any of the theatre companies discussed above simply giving up their broader ambitions when confronted with the intractability of problems of insight and meaning, which they indeed all appear to be fully alert to, especially in the context of the digital. In fact, in each of our performance examples, a tricky double consciousness is apparent. In the performance works, the theatre companies express and explore complex theatrical and digital themes, with particular focus on the ambiguities of digital information and communication. And yet, in their larger conceptions of their projects, and in their assertions of their overall theatre-entrepreneurial mission, they continue to orient themselves around ordered ideas and coherent ambitions, mostly through an embrace of the digital as an accessible resource and a technological good fortune. Foreman perceives philosophically principled theatre as hopelessly (perhaps productively) mired in its own fraught condition, an endlessly unsettled conflict between theatre artists who grasp at challenging insights and theatre audiences who are too easily satisfied with sociable exchange. Wilfully, though not evasively, twenty-first-century theatre groups like the Electric Company, FuturePerfect, and Neworld Theatre have sought to confront, even potentially resolve, this conflict. A peace settlement is somehow being arrived at, seemingly without conceding any terms.

A common core of values and practices is actually shared by Foreman and these twenty-first-century theatre companies. Most essentially, Foreman's 'total theatre' assumes the same virtues of experiencing alternative (or opposed) perspectives, and – what should come as no surprise at this point – he also encourages the strategic use of multimedia forms and digital technologies as a means to 'disorient received ideas and open the doors for alternative models of perception, organization, and understanding' (see Foreman's mission statement at www.ontological.com/mission.html). But core differences are glaringly evident, too. Foreman's mission statement, unlike the other theatre company statements, is about himself as an artist: presented (awkwardly) in third-person assertions, it tells us about *his* 'trademark' project and *his* 'style', and what *he* 'engages in' and 'seeks to' accomplish in his works. The individually gifted artist, on his own quest, takes the place here of the collaboratively networked group, on a collective mission. Also, in his emphasis on 'uncertainties, mysteries, doubts' (citing the poet John Keats), Foreman valorizes an aesthetic of disorientation and an eschewing of all explanatory frameworks. The valour of such principles comes from remaining in a state of intellectual selflessness, keeping open the doors 'for alternative models of perception, organization, and understanding' (Keats' idea of negative capability). But, although we have heard similar assertions before, for Foreman the achievement of such an intellectual state is an end in itself. In our selected examples of theatre and the digital, a coming to uncertainty instead prompts reevaluation, and then something active – art making, discovery, sociability, civic engagement. Foreman's 'total theatre' ends in sceptically intense self-assessment, while the Electric Company, FuturePerfect, and Neworld Theatre continue on, in different ways, towards eager, wilful adumbrations of cultural enterprise and engaged social practice.

To be fair, in actuality Foreman is himself an incredibly active collaborator and important theatre entrepreneur. Still, it is safe to say that he would be virulently opposed to the broad, solution-oriented assumptions of these theatre and the digital projects. FuturePerfect most closely aligns with Foreman's 'total theatre' principles, compelled by, in founding director Wayne Ashley's words, a vantage point of 'ambiguity, circularity, and no finality'. But the outcomes of 'discovery', 'new relationships', and 'possible dialogues' pursued by FuturePerfect would seem to presume the opposite of Foreman's principles of disorientation, alienation, and productive hostility. The notion of a solution-oriented theatre would likely be rejected by FuturePerfect ('we wanted to get away', Ashley says, 'from previous ideas about the coupling of "future" and "technology" as markers of the "new," "better," and "predictable" '), but much of their actual theatre work comes much closer to the empirical – experiments in performance installation and group activity – than the experimental avant-garde tradition that Foreman represents. *Shuffle*, for instance, is specifically an experiment in insight *generation*, bringing together the machine, the theatrical, and the social; the truth-procedures are collective, not subjective. Although as an audience member you can certainly end up feeling a bit dumb and awkward trying to make sense of *Shuffle*, you are always meant to remain fully aware that you are not alone: 'On both sides of the fourth wall', according to the *New Yorker* review of *Shuffle*, 'was a nagging awkwardness' (Henig, 'Hemingway, Faulkner, and Fitzgerald: The Remix'). If there is 'overwhelming information' to be had in 'coded form', the theatre makers and performers are just as oblivious as you are. Collaborative artistic production and collaborative artistic reception are two sides of the same coin.

Provoking audiences or even just trying to reach them one-to-one clashes with what has become a signature of the digital, the ideal of a networked, collective intelligence. Maggie Nelson, one of the more convincing current defenders of the theatre of cruelty principle, partly because of her insistence on the reasonableness and humaneness that, as she sees it, have always been part of the theory, chooses to withhold opinion on one new trend in contemporary art – that which, in her summing up, 'goes by the name of relational aesthetics (or conversational art, or social practice, or community-based art, or littoral art, or … "dialogical" art)' (*The Art of Cruelty*, p. 5). Art as social practice – that is, not art that is *about* social practice, but art that *is* a sort of social practice, typically involving collaborative engagement and interactive story building – does not fall into the general category of 'good-intentioned, activist, "compassionate" art', despite tending to believe in all those things. For Nelson, this is because the activist problems of 'being patronizing, ineffective, or exploitative' do not apply in the usual ways; relational theatre practice is by no means immune to such problems, it is just not doomed from the start (p. 9). Such theatre-cultural projects, according to Nelson, 'follow a different trajectory altogether' from either the cruel (Foreman: 'hostile') or compassionate ('loving') forms that critics like her or theatre theorists like Foreman tend to think between. Nelson also notes that the trend towards relational art practices may be reviving old ideas of progress achieved through the arts, possibly with more 'viable' (her word) models than either the Enlightenment or early twentieth-century arts vanguardism had at their disposal. 'There is much to admire here,' Nelson concludes, 'as well as much to question' (p. 5). She leaves it there.

Our final example of theatre and the digital, The Mission Business's *ZED.TO* (Fringe Toronto, 2012), offers solutions all around: a solution to the problems of insularity and narcissism raised by the Electric Company Theatre's *At Home With Dick and Jane*; a solution to the arbitrariness of ERS/FuturePerfect's *Shuffle*, while also making use of that project's generative, combinatory methods of invention and discovery; and a solution to the deferral of actual sociability and civic engagement, the question that Neworld

Theatre's PodPlays project leaves unanswered. *ZED.TO* also has good answers to Nelson's concerns about activist art being 'patronizing, ineffective, or exploitative'; but, as Nelson predicts, the solutions might end up tipping us over into a new set of troubling problems.

Let's start here: instead of the usual sources of public and private arts funding (although it had some of that, too), the metacultural pathway that The Mission Business took to create initial interest in and support for *ZED.TO* was through the online crowd-funding site Indiegogo. Those who sponsored the project online – 333 people did so – also simultaneously performed a part in it. In reality, the Indiegogo contributors were sponsoring the theatre company; in an alternative reality, they were participating in the performance itself, taking the role of venture capitalists funding the biotech start-up ByoLogyc. The real-world constraint of needing to fund the theatre project provided a dramatic prologue to the play, taking place (in real time) about two years before the final curtain.

The 'live' performance of the play took eight months to act out. The actors and the audience, as in the funding scheme, were one and the same. Both online and at real-world sites around the city of Toronto (at a nightclub, at a wellness clinic, at an industrial site), up to 3,500 people at a time would come together to act out, and thereby shape, the company story of ByoLogyc. Broadly, the story is about the company's production of a ByoRenew pill that threatens human annihilation. To know the full particulars of the story, however, would be impossible: even the theatre company members are, still today, unaware of large parts of the dialogue and action, even though that dialogue and that action constitute the primary relationships between character and influence major outcomes in the plot. In that sense, the audience not only performs the play but also co-creates it, from different angles and with different levels of interest. Adding to the complexity is the online component: character relationships (both real relationships and play relationships), company planning (real storyboarding and play company building), and contextualization (real audience response to the play and play-world response to the events) continuously evolved 'live' online during the eight-month performance. The online performance included creative and 'official' social media use (twitter.com/byologyc/lists/byostaff; www.drakevisitations.com/byologycapp/), an interactive product 'lab' (vip.byologyc.com), an anarchic message board (www.exeishere.org/x/), and an official corporate website (www.byologyc.com), developed through the 'work' of corporate-side audience-participants. The main production website, which continues to carry on the fiction of the play, is at zed.to.

The Mission Business calls what they do a cross between team building, interactive theatre, cross-media engagement, design, entertainment experience, and future casting; instead of a theatre company, they refer to themselves as an 'adventure laboratory' (twitter.com/themissionbiz; also see www.themission.biz). The 'Business'-end of The Mission Business is both entrepreneurial and a frame of ideology critique. Entrepreneurially, The Mission Business organizes creative corporate team-building seminars and retreats, and believes that their performance methods could be applied to the innovation and design of better businesses in the real world, starting from the ground up. Artistically, they are attempting to critique corporate and consumer culture by 'studying' (their word, as opposed to 'provoking' or 'revealing') the personal motives, group dynamics, and cultural assumptions behind future bad decisions in the public, private, and corporate sectors. For instance, another monetization-as-performance-element of *ZED. TO* was their tiered ticketing system: for the final offline performance event, the more an audience-participant paid for their ticket, the more corporate standing and institutional influence they acquired – from a low-level evacuee whose main experience of the story is as a passive victim (as a mere spectator), to a high-ranking ByoLogyc board member or well-funded saboteur whose experience is much more active, empowered, and imposing (more director or creator of the story than spectator). The hypothesis of this artistic research was that higher buy-in (buying the higher-priced tickets) would correlate with a higher degree of interest and engagement in the role playing, whereas the audience at lower price points would be satisfied with, or at least accepting of, a mass spectatorship experience. The analogies between the tiered ticketing system and issues of class, capital, and professional hegemony are obvious, but also tricky. The relatively small number of performers and audience-participants at the upper end might have a different sense of story control and privileged access to information, but their limited awareness of broader currents and felt concerns kept them outside their own story in crucial ways. Likewise, the crowd could counterplot at will, tactically-defensively responding to the strategic-proactive decisions of others; a different sort of agency could be experienced, and different 'real' kinds of relationship between audience-participants could be achieved.

Social media, especially for the crowd, extended the story world and the interconnective community-building experiment into an online performance experience, producing alternating moments of revolutionary consciousness, trivial indifference, and overwhelming randomness. The boundary between corporate leader (responsible or villainous) and citizen activist (responsible or anarchist) was blurred. Online acts such as sharing information ('story data', as perceived from a creative outlook), organizing groups, blogging, viral marketing, and using interactive tools to innovate and bridge institutional divisions – not only were these deemed part of the 'live' performance itself; they directly determined the nature of the narrative form and theatrical experience. *ZED.TO* is an example of artistic research and relational theatre practice, but, in that case, it is as dependent on the digital as it is on the social for its identity and practice: interconnectivity functions as performance, and performance functions as interconnectivity.

Also, finally, *ZED.TO* is about play. The Mission Business is interested in the paired goals of solving problems and disrupting routine thinking, yet the spirit of doing so is 'playful collaboration' (www.themission.biz). The intent of playfulness is meant to evade artistic narcissism, while the open model of collaborative performance frees the project from insularity. The collective devising of the story keeps intentionality and motive present in the work; the dynamics of offline and online production of 'story data', however, are always partly randomized, adaptive, and provisional. And the live, interactive experiences and cross-media engagements that constitute the overall theatrical performance also demand real relationship building, creative thinking, and social and political problem solving. Bridging theatre and the digital for The Mission Business is about bringing 'a much-needed dose of creativity and social collaboration to a domain of increasing importance – the study and design of better futures' (Trevor Haldenby blog interview with Elize Morgan, 'Post-ARGs: ZedTO, Visitations and the Mission Biz', 31 March 2013, www.elizemorgan.com/2013/03/post-args-zedto-visitations-and-mission.html). Progress in solving social and cultural problems comes for the theatre first by way of solving its own problems. A wager on a better future is the same kind of wager as wanting to develop a more strategic, innovative, visionary model of theatre. The digital is both a creative tool and prime motive for such problem solving; it is also one of the problems needing to be solved.

Conclusion

At the Salon Suisse 2013 arts conference, a collateral event with the Venice Biennale, a surprising theme was decided on: the legacy of the Enlightenment in the contemporary art world. The surprise was to hear 'Enlightenment', which has long been associated with haughty idealism and rational positivism, being discussed as a fundamental source and standard for contemporary art, typically prized for its radical conceptualism and sheer irrationalism. In the Salon Suisse event programme, the art historian and journalist Jörg Scheller comments:

> 'Enlightenment'? Isn't this a worn-out concept of the 18th-century – way too idealistic, Eurocentric, and self-righteous in the face of today's globalized, hybrid cultures? And hasn't the postmodern philosophy dismantled the high hopes of Enlightenment…? Well, I wish things were so easy. In fact, many of the problems that the 18th century grappled with have resurfaced and are fiercely contested – for instance, the relationships between religion and politics, freedom of speech and criticism, or the role of art in science and society. The belief that art will transform life for the better was seminal for the Enlightenment. And in one way or another, we still adhere to this creed – banks, when they build art collections; cities, when they finance public art; governments, when they support 'artistic research'. ('Introduction', Salon Suisse event programme, 2013, pp. 7–8, issuu.com/artupdate/docs/programme_salon_suisse_2013)

Scheller explicitly draws out what I believe undergirds all the theatre and the digital examples we have been discussing in this book: the fact that artistic activity is dependent for its identity on the cultural institutions and metacultural phenomena circulating around it. Although art, like reason, cannot solve the problems that trouble us with any completeness or finality, our culture continues to place it in the privileged position of representing our highest hopes. For Scheller, recognizing this arrangement between art and culture means needing to take seriously the problem of 'how to develop new forms of Enlightenment beyond naïve belief in progress, humanism or multiculturalism' (p. 8). As Scheller admits, this is a 'big question, for sure. Too big? Well, from my point of view, questions can never be too big. It's just that mostly our answers are not big enough' (p. 8). It is the premise of this book that the capaciousness of the digital is currently giving new scope to the artistic and cultural project of theatre. That new scope, I would argue, is a triumph of progress in itself.

further reading

The Internet is the obvious place of first resort for those interested in theatre and the digital. Many theatre company websites offer provocative but often usefully simplified accounts of theoretical engagements and performance methodologies; also, in addition to YouTube, these websites are a good place to find video clips of performance works. Other than the main examples discussed in this book – the Electric Company Theatre (electriccompanytheatre.com), FuturePerfect (futureperfectproductions.org), Neworld Theatre (www.neworldtheatre.com), and The Mission Business (zed.to) – great websites are hosted by Blast Theory (www.blasttheory.co.uk), The Builders Association (www.thebuildersassociation.org), Ex Machina (www.lacaserne.net), and 3-Legged Dog (www.3leggeddog.org/mt/).

Innovation and intervention in the arts typically relies on funding from arts councils and charities, and the websites of these funding groups can often be very useful informational resources as well. The UK-based charity Nesta — formerly NESTA, the National Endowment for Science, Technology and the Arts — recently conducted a study, *Beyond Live*, of digital strategies for public arts engagement, taking the National Theatre Live project as its primary case study (www.nesta.org.uk/publications/beyond-live). Theatre Sandbox is a commissioning and development initiative supported by Arts Council England that specifically promotes the use of 'pervasive media technologies' in the theatre arts (www.watershed.co.uk/ished/theatresandbox). In the United States, the non-profit arts organization Creative Capital provides similar support for a range of funding, arts research, and entrepreneurship initiatives, likewise emphasizing the importance of digital strategies (www.creative-capital.org). Contact is a globally minded arts charity that itself makes use of digital innovation principles and development strategies to help young artists to become creative leaders and community activists (contactmcr.com).

Studies on theatre and the digital fall into one of two kinds. Survey books are the main kind: Steve Dixon's *Digital Performance* (2007), probably the broadest-ranging but still theoretically tractable compendium on the topic, is an especially energizing and enlivening introduction to the field. A more recent compendium, *Mapping Intermediality in Performance* (2010), edited by Sarah Bay-Cheng, Chiel Kattenbelt, Andy Lavender, and Robin Nelson, charts different forms of mixed-media performance; the book is available open access through OAPEN (www.oapen.org). Gabriella Giannchi's *Virtual Theatres: An Introduction* (2004),

Jennifer-Parker Starbuck's *Cyborg Theatre: Corporeal/Technological Intersections in Multimedia Performance* (2011), and Rosemary Klich and Edward Scheer's *Multimedia Performance* (2012) all attempt to narrow down what is meant by digital theatre — focusing on what they term 'virtual theatre', 'cyborg theatre', and 'multimedia performance', respectively — and then survey within those more specified paradigms, providing much needed models for interpretation, as well as helpful perspective for historical research. Chris Salter's *Entangled: Technology and the Transformation of Performance* (2010) is another critical source book of this sort, but with the assumption of a much more capacious, roving concept of performance.

Another kind of study tends more towards the abstractly theoretical. In these studies, the digital is typically analysed as a deep cultural or aesthetic logic, rather than as a type of performance work. Matthew Causey's *Theatre and Performance in Digital Culture* (2006), for instance, explores the problems of identity in our data-driven digital culture and then applies those considerations to the possibilities of performance. More abstractly, Brian Massumi's *Parables of the Virtual* (2002) attempts to reconfigure how we think about bodily experience and expression as a cultural fact, with chapters on Ronald Reagan's acting career and the Australian performance artist Stelarc. Touching on the digital but not focusing solely on it, Baz Kershaw's *Theatre Ecology: Environments and Performance Events* (2008) offers probably the most positive endorsement of the digital as a way forward for theatre and the performing arts (Causey,

on the other hand, is probably the most cautiously negative). Finally, almost any work on theatre and the digital
eventually comes around to the debate between Peggy
Phelan and Philip Auslander over the concepts of 'liveness'
and 'mediation', in their respective books *Unmarked: The
Politics of Performance* (1993) and *Liveness: Performance in
a Mediatized Culture* (1997, 2nd ed. 2008). Both concepts
have been challenged and rethought many times over since
these books were first published, but having such a clear
origin point for a critical debate is unique and very much
worth tracing back to.

A way around the inevitably rapid datedness of making
claims about theatre and new media as new media is continuously innovated has been to publish in scholarly journals
rather than books. The journal *Theater* devoted a special
issue to 'Digital Dramaturgies' in 2012. *Theatre Journal*'s
December 2009 issue is on 'Digital Media and Performance'.
The *International Journal of Performance Arts and Digital Media*
has been publishing quarterly since 2005. *Scan: Journal of
Media Arts* has been publishing online since 2004.

Digital theatre scholarship can refer to how such scholarship is written, in addition to what it is written about. *The
Drama Review* recently announced a plan to start publishing
born-digital, multimodal scholarly articles; the first of these
articles, 'Hearing the Music of the Hemispheres' by Erin
Mee, can be found online at scalar.usc.edu/anvc/music-of-
the-hemispheres/index. In a similar vein, the performance
scholar Jon McKenzie has been publishing video essays on his
own website (www.labster8.net) for the past few years.

Analyses of community engagement in the arts have been numerous of late, and typically include at least some discussion of how digital seems to hold out a special promise on these fronts. Shannon Jackson's 2011 book *Social Works: Performing Art, Supporting Publics* is likely to become a primary reference for critical discussions on this topic for the near future. Other recent books that negotiate between the discourse and practice of cultural engagement in the arts, both positively and sceptically, include Arlene Goldbard, *New Creative Community: The Art of Cultural Development* (2006); Michael McKinnie, *City Stages: Theatre and Urban Space in a Global City* (2007); Jill Dolan, *Utopia in Performance: Finding Hope at the Theater* (2005); Baz Kershaw, *The Politics of Performance: Radical Theatre as Cultural Intervention* (1992); and Alan Read, *Theatre, Intimacy, and Engagement: The Last Human Venue* (2008).

As a way to keep up with current theatre projects that variously relate to the digital, the community website Digitalarti (www.digitalarti.com) maintains an events calendar, a news page, a reviews section, and an artists' forum on research and practice in the digital arts, including the performing arts.

Ackroyd, Judith. 'Applied Theatre: Problems and Possibilities.' *Applied Theatre Researcher* 1 (2000). 8 Sept. 2013. <http://www.griffith.edu.au/__data/assets/pdf_file/0004/81796/Ackroyd.pdf >.

Artaud, Antonin. *Selected Writings*. Berkeley: U of California P, 1976.

Auslander, Philip. 'Live from Cyberspace: or, I was sitting at my computer this guy appeared he thought I was a bot.' *Performing Arts Journal* 24.1 (2002): 16–21.

———. *Liveness: Performance in a Mediatized Culture*. 2nd ed. London: Routledge, 2008.

Bakhshi, Hasan, Juan Mateos-Garcia, and David Throsby. *Beyond Live: Digital Innovation in the Performing Arts*. London: NESTA, 2010. 18 Sept. 2013. <www.nesta.org.uk/publications/beyond-live>.

Bay-Cheng, Sarah, Chiel Kattenbelt, Andy Lavender, and Robin Nelson, eds. *Mapping Intermediality in Performance*. Amsterdam: Amsterdam UP, 2010.

Berghaus, Günter. *Avant-Garde Performance: Live Events and Electronic Technologies*. Basingstoke, UK: Palgrave Macmillan, 2005.

Bharucha, Rustom. *Theatre and the World: Performance and the Politics of Culture*. London: Routledge, 1993.

Birringer, Johannes. 'Contemporary Performance/Technology.' *Theatre Journal* 51 (1999): 361–81.

———. *Media and Performance: Along the Border*. Baltimore, MD: Johns Hopkins UP, 1998.

Bishop, Claire. *Artificial Hells: Participatory Art and the Politics of Spectatorship*. London: Verso, 2012.

Bourriaud, Nicolas. *Relational Aesthetics*. Dijon: Les Presses du Réel, 1998.

Brecht, Bertolt. *Brecht on Theatre*. Trans. and ed. John Willett. New York: Hill and Wang, 1964.

Broadhurst, Susan, and Josephine Machon. *Identity, Performance and Technology: Practices of Empowerment, Embodiment and Technicity*. Basingstoke, UK: Palgrave Macmillan, 2012.

Browning, Barbara. *I'm Trying to Reach You*. Columbus, OH: Two Dollar Radio, 2011.

Causey, Matthew. *Theatre and Performance in Digital Culture: From Simulation to Embeddedness*. London: Routledge, 2006.

Cohen-Cruz, Jan. *Local Acts: Community-Based Performance in the United States*. New Brunswick, NJ: Rutgers UP, 2005.

Dixon, Steve. *Digital Performance: A History of New Media in Theater, Dance, Performance Art, and Installation*. Cambridge, MA: MIT Press, 2007.

Dolan, Jill. *Utopia in Performance: Finding Hope at the Theater*. Ann Arbor: U of Michigan P, 2005.

Farman, Jason. 'Surveillance Spectacles: The Big Art Group's Flicker and the Screened Body in Performance.' *Contemporary Theatre Review* 19.2 (2009): 181–94.

Foreman, Richard. *Unbalancing Acts: Foundations for a Theatre*. New York: Theatre Communications Group, 1993.

Giannchi, Gabriella. *Virtual Theatres: An Introduction*. New York: Routledge, 2004.

Gitelman, Lisa. *Always Already New: Media, History, and the Data of Culture*. Cambridge, MA: MIT Press, 2006.

Goldbard, Arlene. *New Creative Community: The Art of Cultural Development*. Oakland, CA: New Village, 2006.

Gomez-Pena, Guillermo. *Ethno-Techno: Writings on Performance, Activism and Pedagogy*. London: Routledge, 2005.

Harries, Martin. 'Theater and Media before "New" Media.' *Theater* 42.2 (2012): 7–25.

Hayles, N. Katherine. 'Intermediation: The Pursuit of a Vision.' *New Literary History* 38.1 (2007): 99–125.

————. *My Mother Was a Computer: Digital Subjects and Literary Texts*. Chicago, IL: U of Chicago P, 2005.

Henig, Samantha. 'Hemingway, Faulkner, and Fitzgerald: The Remix.' *The New Yorker* 25 May 2011. Online. <http://www.newyorker.com/online/blogs/books/2011/05/hemingway-faulkner-and-fitzgerald-the-remix.html>.

Jackson, Shannon. *Social Works: Performing Art, Supporting Publics*. New York: Routledge, 2011.

Kershaw, Baz. *The Politics of Performance: Radical Theatre as Cultural Intervention*. New York: Routledge, 1992.

————. *Theatre Ecology: Environments and Performance Events*. Cambridge: Cambridge UP, 2008.

Klich, Rosemary. 'Send: Act: Perform.' *Performance Research* 18.5 (2013): 117–23.

Klich, Rosemary, and Edward Scheer. *Multimedia Performance*. Basingstoke, UK: Palgrave Macmillan, 2012.

Kustow, Michael. *theatre@risk*. 2nd ed. London: Methuen, 2001.

Lehmann, Hans-Thies. *Postdramatic Theatre*. Trans. Karen Jurs-Munby. New York: Routledge, 2006.

Massumi, Brian. *Parables of the Virtual*. Durham, NC: Duke UP, 2002.

McKinnie, Michael. *City Stages: Theatre and Urban Space in a Global City*. Toronto: U of Toronto P, 2007.

Melrose, Susan, and Nick Hunt. 'Techne, Technology, Technician: The Creative Practices of the Mastercraftsperson.' *Performance Research: A Journal of Performing Arts* 10.4 (2005): 70–82.

Milne, Esther. *Letters, Postcards, Email: Technologies of Presence.* New York: Routledge, 2010.

Munster, Anna. *Materialising New Media: Embodiment in Information Aesthetics.* Hanover, NH: Dartmouth College Press, 2006.

Murray, Janet. *Hamlet on the Holodeck: The Future of Narrative in Cyberspace.* New York: Free Press, 1997.

Muse, John. '140 Characters in Search of a Theater: Twitter Plays.' *Theater* 42.2 (2012): 43–63.

Nelson, Maggie. *The Art of Cruelty.* New York: Norton, 2011.

Nicholson, Helen. *Applied Drama: The Gift of Theatre.* New York: Palgrave Macmillan, 2005.

Nielsen, Michael. *Reinventing Discovery: The New Era of Discovery.* Princeton, NJ: Princeton UP, 2011.

Phelan, Peggy. *Unmarked: The Politics of Performance.* New York: Routledge, 1993.

Popat, Sita. *Invisible Connections: Dance, Choreography and Internet Communities.* New York: Routledge, 2006.

Rayner, Alice. 'Everywhere and Nowhere: Theatre in Cyberspace.' *Of Borders and Thresholds: Theatre History, Practice and Theory.* Ed. Michael Kobialka. Minneapolis: U of Minnesota P, 1999. 278–302.

Read, Alan. *Theatre, Intimacy, and Engagement: The Last Human Venue.* Basingstoke, UK: Palgrave Macmillan, 2008.

Ricardo, Francisco. *Literary Art in Digital Performance: Case Studies in New Media Art and Criticism.* New York: Continuum, 2009.

Salter, Chris. *Entangled: Technology and the Transformation of Performance.* Cambridge, MA: MIT Press, 2010.

Saltz, David. 'Digital Literary Studies: Performance and Interaction.' *A Companion to Digital Literary Studies.* Ed. Ray Siemens. Malden, MA: Blackwell, 2007. 336–48.

———. 'Performing Arts.' *A Companion to Digital Humanities.* Ed. Susan Schreibman, Ray Siemens, and John Unsworth. Malden, MA: Blackwell, 2004. 121–31.

Shaughnessy, Nicola. *Applying Performance: Live Art, Socially Engaged Theatre and Affective Practice*. Basingstoke, UK: Palgrave Macmillan, 2012.

Starbuck, Jennifer-Parker. *Cyborg Theatre: Corporeal/Technological Intersections in Multimedia Performance*. New York: Palgrave Macmillan, 2011.

Stocking, George. *Victorian Anthropology*. New York: Free Press, 1987.

Taylor, Diana. *The Archive and the Repertoire: Performing Cultural Memory in the Americas*. Durham, NC: Duke UP, 2003.

Thompson, James. *Applied Theatre: Bewilderment and Beyond*. New York: Peter Lange, 2003.

Urban, Greg. *Metaculture: How Culture Moves through the World*. Minneapolis: U of Minnesota P, 2001.

Vanderbeeken, Robrecht, Boris De Backere, and Christel Stalpaert, eds. *Bastard or Playmate? Adapting Theatre, Mutating Media and Contemporary Performing Arts*. Amsterdam: Amsterdam UP, 2011.

Vanhoutte, Kurt, and Nele Wynants. 'Immersion.' *Mapping Intermediality in Performance*. Ed. Sarah Bay-Cheng, Chiel Kattenbelt, Andy Lavender, and Robin Nelson. Amsterdam: Amsterdam UP, 2010. 47.

Wilson-Bokowiec, Julie. 'Sense and Sensation: The Act of Mediation and Its Effects.' *Intermediality: History and Theory of the Arts, Literature and Technologies* 12 (2008): 129–42.

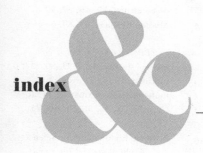

index

acknowledgements

M uch of my thinking in this book took place alongside collaborations with the Re:Enlightenment Project. I would like to thank all the Re:Enlightenment collaborators, particularly the project leaders, Clifford Siskin, Peter De Bolla, William Warner, and Leslie Santos Siskin. In the Dramatic Literature programme at New York University, thank you to my friends and colleagues Una Chaudhuri, Martin Harries, Julia Jarcho, and Erin Mee. Also providing an impetus for this book was the Digital Commons Initiative, a partnership between the Department of English and NYU Libraries; many great conversations with Thomas Augst, Kevin Brine, Lisa Gitelman, David Hoover, Monica McCormick, and Jennifer Vinopal led to a number of timely, sustaining insights. I would also like to acknowledge the series editors, Jen Harvie and Dan Rebellato, and the team at Palgrave Macmillan, especially Jenni Burnell, for their enthusiasm and support in seeing this book through to completion.

A turning point in my writing came during a weekend trip to Toronto in April 2013. I had the chance that weekend to meet with Trevor Haldenby, Byron Laviolette, and Elena Mosoff of The Mission Business; our many-sided chat about foresight, futures, and theatre history helped to give greater scope to my thinking on this topic. The trip was special for another reason, too, as we were in Toronto for the first birthday of my nieces, Audrey and Olivia. Many thanks to Kim and Dan Farmer, both for my nieces and for Friday night pizza. Also, continual thanks to my parents, who joined us for some adventuring that weekend, which they are always up for, whenever, wherever; such parents, with all our many travels together, make everything seem possible, practical, and within reach.

And to Ginger, my truest reader and friend.